Grades K-3 Book Two
Stories of Artists and Their Art

Written by Brenda Ellis
Edited by Ariel DeWitt and Daniel D. Ellis
Cover, book design, and illustrations by Brenda Ellis
Students' works were created in art classes Mrs. Ellis taught from 2002-2008.

Second Edition

ACKNOWLEDGMENTS

Thanks to all the students who participated in the lessons and to those who let us share their work with others through this book. Thanks to Christine Ann Feorino for editing the first edition of this book. Thanks to Dover Publications Inc., NY and Art Resources, NY for supplying the fine art images by the great masters.

Copyright © 2003, 2005, 2007, 2008 by Brenda Ellis

All rights reserved. No portion of this book may be reproduced – mechanically, electronically, or by any other means, including photocopying. Please don't compromise the educational value of this book by photocopying images. Children cannot see what a pencil drawing or color work should look like when color and tonal values are reduced to black and white.

Printed in the U.S.A.

ISBN 978-0-9815982-2-2

Published by
Artistic Pursuits Inc.
Northglenn, Colorado
www.artisticpursuits.com
alltheanswers@artisticpursuits.com

Contents

Page	Lesson	
3		Materials
4		Introduction
7	1	Cimabue
10	2	*Madonna Enthroned, with Saints and Angels*
12	3	Giotto
15	4	*Lamentation of Christ*
17	5	Limbourg
20	6	*August (Departure for the Falcon Hunt)*
22	7	Van Eyck
25	8	*Jean Arnolfini and His Wife*
26	9	Leonardo da Vinci
29	10	*Mona Lisa*
31	11	Michelangelo
33	12	*Delphic Sibyl*
35	13	Raphael
38	14	*Portrait of a Young Woman (Lady with a Unicorn)*
40	15	Anguissola
42	16	*Three Sisters Playing Chess*
44	17	Durer
46	18	*Flight to Egypt*
50	19	Bruegel
52	20	*Hunters in the Snow*
54	21	Parmigianino
56	22	*The Conversion of Paul*
58	23	Rembrandt
60	24	*Abraham's Sacrifice*
62	25	Vermeer
64	26	*The Artist in his Studio*
66	27	Fragonard
68	28	*A Young Girl Reading*
70	29	Turner
72	30	*The Fighting Temeraire*
74	31	Millet
76	32	*The Gleaners*
79		Bibliography

Materials

The materials needed for this book are listed in groups. Each project tells you the group number so that you will know what you need to complete the project by referring to this page. Having these items on hand will make preparation for each art class simple.

GROUP #1 PAINTING

- 1- Prang pan watercolor set of eight colors or more
- 1- Tempera paint set of six colors or more
- 1- Round watercolor brush, size #6 or #8
- 1- Flat watercolor brush ¼ inch
- 1- Watercolor paper pad
- 10- Sheets of cardboard or chipboard
- 1- Small 8oz. Spackling paste
- 1- Small plastic putty knife

GROUP #2 DRAWING

- 1- Ebony pencil
- 1- Set of 16 oil pastels (*CrayPas* preferred)
- 1- Drawing pad
- 1- Stylus (scratch tool) or nail

GROUP #3 PRINTMAKING

- 1- Brayer
- 2- Water-soluble printing ink (black or colors)
- 10- Styrofoam sheets for printmaking
- 2- Craft foam sheets, 2mm thick, any color

GROUP #4 MODELING

- 1- Box of instant **papier-mâché**, 1 lb
- 2- Plastic knife
- 1- Pointed stick

GROUP #5 MIXED MEDIA

- 1- Package construction paper
- 1- Package tissue paper
- 1- natural sponge
- 1- Scissors (Fiskars preferred)

Additional Items Needed

Masking tape, paper towels, water containers, wax paper, apple, lemon juice, salt, sock, cardboard tube, Dixie cup, paper plates, bright cotton cloth 12 x 12 inches, Elmer's Glue-All.

Teaching Observation Skills

As you ponder the best approach to teaching art, consider the benefits of working directly from nature. Copying an adult model from the pages of a book is a meager offering when compared to the variety of subjects available in nature. The child who copies the adult model will gain skills required to repeat that model, but the nature observer will gain so much more. The child spending time in direct observation of nature will develop technical skills, personal preferences for certain types of subject matter, awareness of details, problem solving skills, awareness of composition, as well as developing a creative approach to life. This book encourages children to observe the world around them and to choose their own subjects. When allowed freedom to explore the possibilities, children will make art without fear and demonstrate the ability to make personal statements.

In each lesson children will look at artists and their artwork, learn new techniques for making art, and engage in a project. What makes some students ready to make art, while others seem void of ideas? Those who jump in have brought something extra to the classroom. It is a wealth of knowledge based on their observations of the world. They draw from what they know, and what they've looked at in the past. In their art, we see their world. A parent of such a child claimed that she had not trained her child in the arts, but she tried to point things out to her boy to get him to observe them more closely. This may be the structure of a flower, a sunset, or the way the ice hangs on the trees to make a winter wonderland. She also showed him artworks by other artists, but they did not talk too much about them due to her lack of knowledge. Another parent said she does nothing special, that the boys draw on their own and draw a lot. Further into the conversation she said that she reads many classic adventure stories to them and made the radical move of giving away the TV. She had supplied her sons with the environment and opportunity to make art. Their days were filled with quiet hours spent dreaming and visualizing heroic adventures. They also posses a natural curiosity for the outdoors. Paper and pencils are available to them at these times. Both of these parents found something bigger than art techniques to share with their children. They presented them with a view of life, and an appreciation for living things. They laid the groundwork for grasping the subject of art.

In this book, your child will explore the lives of artists who gave us a vision of the world that has inspired people for generations. *Grades K-3 Book 2, Stories of Artists and Their Art* is a continuation of the ancient art history section in *Grades K-3 Book 1, An Introduction to the Visual Arts.* It focuses on unique projects, which give students opportunities to make original works of art. Units are based on individual artists within major periods of art. The purpose of the text is to place in students' minds the primary character of each artist and his work through short fictional stories. Each artist has given us a unique vision of the world he or she lived in. Students can come to know that vision and apply it to their own creative works. Students have always learned

from the artwork of past artists. Charlotte Mason expresses the value of looking at art of the past.

> We cannot measure the influence that one or another artist has upon the child's sense of beauty, upon his power of seeing, as in a picture, the common sights of life: he is enriched more than we know in having really looked at even a single picture. – Charlotte M. Mason, *Home Education*, 309.

In the field of teaching, where there is so much pressure to measure through testing, can we dare to offer our children a rich body of knowledge in which we cannot measure the true depth of the outcome? Can we dare to trust that a natural curiosity about the world is worth the time a child invests in it? We cannot measure the influence that close contact with nature has on the child's ability to make beautiful art. Art is the expression of life. We, who may have been taught to color within the lines, to use "correct" colors, and follow all rules spoken from the teacher's viewpoint, must abandon that meager helping of knowledge. These rules are only helpful when they are applied to nature in order to see it more clearly. The outcomes of studying from nature are difficult to measure through testing, although with time the benefits are clearly seen.

It takes a bit of faith to trust that the outcome of our child's art will be better when time is spent in nature. My children have walked that path and many others have as well. I cherished the freedom my children had to explore the world not only by planned activities like trips to the park to draw birds, but the unplanned adventures as well. Large rainstorms meant a recess was in order. We watched the storm build and then put the books down, ran outdoors, and spun around in the rain. A big snowfall meant that morning would be devoted to play. Afterward, our minds invigorated, we settled down to a warm meal, dry clothing, and school subjects as the sun melted our snowmen.

Some parents choose to avoid nature for the sake of cleanliness. In my classes, it is those that worry about messy hands that are afraid to make art. Their fears interfere with the mental freedom it takes to conceive of a picture. Yes, children get wet, dirty, and messy when allowed to enjoy the outdoors. They also are filled up inside with an appreciation for the world. They acquire knowledge of what it feels like to have cold hands, run in rain-soaked clothing, or dig into soft earth with a small shovel. Their minds work as they invent ingenious ways to get large amounts of sand from one part of the lawn to the next. Well-manicured lawns may suffer a bit, but those are easily repaired. I have not been particularly fussy about what the kids do in the yard. When they wanted a mud hole, I told them where they could make it, and later turned the bald patch into a flowerbed.

Children need nature if they are to become creative individuals. They need to experience it, manipulate it, and gain some knowledge and control over

it. They then bring the knowledge they've gained to every experience they encounter. If its art, they make it well. They treat their art as they treat the world. They experience it, manipulate it, and gain knowledge and control over it. Children benefit in knowing how to handle the materials they come in contact with in art. Children who learn to see the world, will find the robin hopping in the yard a fascinating part of their own world and worthy of including it in their next artwork. An art program should first point the child to nature as a good teacher in the visual arts. It can then present the use of art materials and technical skills, once an acquaintance of nature is firmly established within the child's methods of creating art.

This picture shows one of many sunny days spent playing in the snow.

I dedicate this book to three wonderfully creative children, Nathaniel, Ariel, and Laurel. They are the delight of my life and it has been sheer joy watching them grow, explore, and become the unique individuals that they were designed to be. Through helping them find their paths, I found my own. Home schooling gave me more time to be with them and I am forever grateful to all those who helped us walk this way.

Lesson 1

Gothic Period

Cimabue
Giovanni Cimabue, *CHEEmah BOO eh,* (~1240-~1302)

Most fairy tales begin with the phrase, "Once upon a time…," and end with the phrase, "And they lived happily ever after." What stories do you know that begin and end this way? These stories are full of knights, young maidens, and magnificent castle towers. Our story is about a real person who lived in just such a time.

Once upon a time children began moving into towns with their families in hopes of finding a safer place to live. However, the feuds and battles that they had hoped to escape from continued even there. So many battles had taken place in the town of Florence, Italy that little was left of their buildings. Wealthy families began to build towers for protection. So many towers were built that the city was a maze of fortresses. The towers became very tall. Men feared that they would no longer be able to see the sky. Children's fathers gathered in groups to discuss the problem. They soon discovered that groups could agree upon actions to solve the problem. They set limits for how tall a tower could be built. They decided that other problems could be solved in groups. Each group set up its own rules. These groups were called guilds. In guilds, they discussed how things were sold, how they should be made, and how to train young boys to take the jobs one day. With rules in place, young boys were given the opportunities to learn skills that could be used for their lifetime. As different guilds worked together much of the fighting stopped.   Cimabue was born during this time of building. When his father sent him to study writing, he "spent the whole day drawing men, horses, houses, and various other fantasies in his books and papers" (Vasari 7). At the same time, painters were called from Greece to work on the Gondi Chapel because no one in Florence knew how to paint. Cimabue skipped school to watch the masters in their work. It was decided that he should study with them. He quickly improved upon their techniques and later became a leading member of the Craftsman's Guild. Soon everyone in Florence was talking about him. Young boys hoped Cimabue could train them to draw and paint. Many boys got their wishes. So our story ends with that old line, "and they lived happily ever after."

7

The people of Florence did live more happily after the guild system was in place. It brought the peace that was needed so that people did not spend so much time protecting themselves. Instead, they could work on making beautiful things for their churches. Cimabue painted in the traditional style of medieval art by filling in shapes with flat areas of color, much like a coloring book is used. However, he began tilting heads to add more emotion. He set in motion a desire to make figures look more real. His students and those that followed took this idea much further. Artists for the following 600 years would aim for a more realistic look in their art, as we will see in this book.

The Craftsman

Craftsmen built and painted altarpieces and other decoration for churches. These altarpieces are pictures located in the front of a church. They were made from wooden panels and could be cut in unusual shapes. Often they were attached by hinges so that three or more panels were seen together. Paintings on panels had several layers. First, wooden planks were cut and glued together. Pieces of canvas cloth were glued onto the wood, and then covered with a coat of gesso or sealer like rabbit skin glue. Craftsmen then drew the picture. They applied real gold to special areas, like halos, and often to the entire background. Gold leaves were taken from a box and pressed onto the surface, which had been covered with red glue. Then the craftsman rubbed the area with a piece of cotton to make it stick. Paint was applied to the rest of the painting with a brush. Indentions were then pounded into the gold surface to reflect light and outline halos, creating patterns.

A craftsman applies gold leaf to a panel painting.

8

Project 1: Watercolor Painting

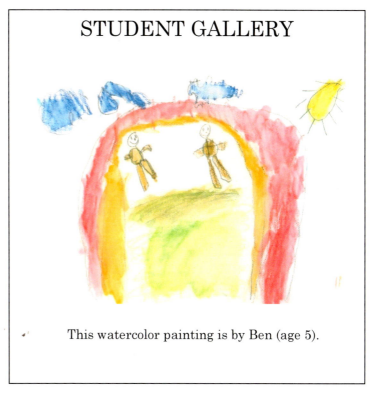

STUDENT GALLERY

This watercolor painting is by Ben (age 5).

> GROUP #1 PAINTING
> - Watercolor paint set
> - Watercolor paper
> - Round brush
> - Water container, paper towel

You can paint like Cimabue. Go for a walk and look at buildings in your neighborhood. Paint a picture of where you live. Set up the paint supplies within easy reach as shown below. Before you begin to paint, dip the brush in water. Hold it over each color allowing a few large drops of water to fall onto the dry color. This softens the paint so that the brush will pick up color easily.

Mix colors in the palette (lid) provided in the watercolor set. Keep colors clean by rinsing the brush each time you use a new color.

Use only the tip of the brush.

Don't smash the bristles!

9

Lesson 2

Madonna Enthroned, with Saints and Angels by Cimabue

Cimabue began drawing and painting people in a more real way than had been seen in the past. He inspired future artists with the same goal, to make figures look real. In this painting, we see the mother of Jesus holding him while seated on a throne. Angles surround them. These winged creatures have halos. The saints line up at the bottom. Cimabue followed many traditions when he made this altarpiece.

Altarpieces showing Madonna and child seated on a throne and surrounded in gold were typical. Cimabue did something new too. He tilted the heads of the Madonna and the angels. This gave the figures a more natural appearance.

How many angels are in the picture?

How many saints are in the picture?

Has Cimabue chosen a natural setting for Jesus and his mother? From what you know about their lives, did they ever sit on a throne?

In the Gothic period, everything in a painting had meaning. What could the throne suggest?

Cimabue, *Madonna Enthroned with Saints and Angels*, c.1280.
Photo Credit: Dover Publications Inc.

Craftsmen often stamped patterns and designs into the gold surface by pounding little indentions into the gold. This textured effect made the painting seem to shimmer as one changed position. You can see these indentions in the throne and Madonna's halo.

10

Project 2: Gold Leaf

GROUP #1 PAINTING
- Watercolor paint set and paper
- Round brush, water container, paper towel
- Gold or yellow paper (Group #5)
- Scissors and glue (Group #5)

STUDENT GALLERY

Gold is used for the castle in this student work by Gemma, (age 9).

Gold leaf is a sheet of real gold that is pounded very thin like a leaf. It is too fragile to work with easily, but you can still make a picture with gold in it. Use gold or yellow paper instead of real gold. (Gold origami sheets can be purchased.)

Cut the gold paper into shapes and glue shapes to your picture. Set up watercolors as shown.

Place the wet brush into one color. The brush will pick up the paint if both the brush and the paint are wet.

Apply the color to watercolor paper. Always pull the brush back and forth, as you paint. Never smash the bristles against the paper or push the brush forward so that the hairs fan out.

Wash the brush when you want to change colors. Wipe the brush on the edge of the water container and go to the next color.

Gothic Period   **Lesson 3**

Giotto   Giotto di Bondone, *JAH toh,* (1267–1337)

Giotto helped his father watch over the sheep. The sheep grazed in green fields all day so Giotto had lots of time as a young boy to think, dream, and to discover. Do you have a place to go where you can think or daydream with no particular purpose in mind? Young Giotto discovered that he had artistic talent in just such a place.

Young Giotto opened the fenced gate. His father's sheep sprung forward, making their way to the best grasses and wild flowers, as they did each day. Giotto followed them and watched for a time, as his shepherd duties demanded. However, like all young boys assigned to such tiresome tasks, he spent most of his day climbing the green hills. He took great leaps from boulders that jutted out from the landscape. He threw stones at small targets he'd carved into huge boulders.

One day, as he picked up a small rock to practice his aim, he noticed that the circles he'd scratched onto the boulders looked like sheep. Giotto gazed at the sheep. Then a great impulse overtook him and turning a rock's sharper edge outward, he began scratching onto a flat stone. He scratched not circles, but sheep! "This is great fun!" he thought. Giotto was amazed at the way lines turned into pictures of the sheep that grazed on the hillside. In the days and years that followed, he filled the boulders with many pictures of sheep. He searched for large flat stones to draw on. These images he carried home with him. Giotto continued this practice each day until his skills became quite good.

One day Cimabue, the famous painter we met in the last story, became curious about the boy who carried the stone tablets. He introduced himself and Giotto showed Cimabue his art on stone. His "talent impressed Cimabue so much that he made Giotto his apprentice" (Rabiner 193). As an apprentice, Giotto worked for Cimabue without pay, while he learned how to paint like an artist. Giotto practiced all that Cimabue taught him. He became a master painter, known for his fresco paintings.

Just as Giotto carefully observed his father's sheep, he carefully observed people. Giotto became well known for his skill in painting people with expression and emotion.

> **What is a fresco painting?**
>
> A fresco is created when paint is applied onto a wet plaster wall. A rough layer of plaster was applied to the stone walls of a church. A second smoother layer was painted over the section that was to be painted that day. The craftsman painted that section before the plaster dried. Because of this technique, one picture has many sections and you can often see these in good reproductions of the works of the time. Since many paintings covered the walls of large church buildings, the craftsmen often had to work on scaffolding, wooden planks that could be put up then taken down to be put in other areas. This illustration shows that the top left section has been completed in a previous day. Giotto and Cimabue start the second section.

Florentine patrons were very proud of how real their artists could make things look. They spread the story of how, as master artist Cimabue was out, young Giotto painted a fly on the nose of a figure Cimabue had been working on. When Cimabue returned, he tried many times to brush the fly away before realizing Giotto's trick. And that was how well Giotto could paint!

Were you fooled by the fly on this page?

13

Project 3: Scratch Art

GROUP #2 DRAWING
- Oil pastels
- Scratch tool
- Chipboard or cardboard (Group #1)

You can make art by scratching into a soft surface just as Giotto did as a young boy. He used rocks and stone. You can use a softer material, oil pastels. Draw a picture of what you imagine Giotto saw as he tended his father's sheep on the grassy hills.

This scratch artwork is by Caleb (age 6). Caleb used bright colors as the first layer, covered the colors in black, and then scratched the horse, clouds, grass, and sun.

Cover one side of a piece of cardboard with a light pastel color such as gray, white, or rust. Press hard on the pastel to make a thick layer of solid color.

Next, color over the first layer using a black pastel. Color first one way, then another, until none of the original color shows through.

Use a nail, paper clip, or scratch tool to scratch the surface. Scratch the main outlines of your picture first. Then fill in parts using wavy lines, wiggly lines, wide lines, and thin lines.

If you like this way of drawing, try using a rainbow of colors under the black layer in your next artwork.

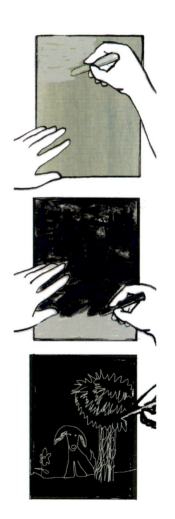

Lesson 4

Lamentation of Christ by Giotto

    Much of the art from Europe during the Gothic period was made for Christian churches. Artists were commissioned to paint stories centering on the life of Christ. Giotto's painting depicts the moment when Christ was taken off the cross. Those who love him mourn his tragic death. Giotto used gold halos (circles around the heads) to show those who were filled with God's light. Artists used the types of materials that the patron, the person paying for the job, requested. Even rarer and more expensive than gold was the blue color used lavishly in all of Giotto's works. This was a magnificent sight for those entering the dark church interior lit by candles. The gold reflected the flickering candlelight and the blue seemed like a color sent from the heavens above.

How many people have halos?

Do the people look sad?

How many figures have wings and halos?

Do these angels seem to feel sorrow too?

How do their postures show their feelings of deep sorrow?

Giotto, *Lamentation of Christ*, c. 1305,
Photo Credit: Dover Publications Inc.

    Artists before Giotto's time painted people stiffly and without expression, but not Giotto. See the difference that gestures make. Look in a mirror. First, hold your body still so that you show no emotions. That is how they painted people. Next, make a face and move your body to show that you are sad. Then, make a face and bend your body to show that you are happy. That is how Giotto painted people. Remember Giotto for painting people that bend, move, and show real emotions.

Project 4: Fresco

> **GROUP #1 PAINTING**
> - Spackling paste
> - Chipboard (cardboard)
> - Watercolor paint set
> - Round brush
> - Water container, paper towel, pencil

STUDENT GALLERY

Lauren (age 9) shows her family seated at the table. She remembers a conversation from the night before.

You can make a fresco just like Giotto, using plaster (also called Spackling paste, available at hardware stores) and paint. Make a scene that shows the emotions of the people in it.

Apply a thin layer of Spackling paste over a piece of cardboard with a putty knife or corner piece of cardboard. Allow the Spackling paste to dry.

Draw a picture with pencil directly onto the plaster surface.

Prepare the watercolor paints by adding a few drops of water to each color. Set up watercolors as shown on page nine.

Paint on the surface just as you paint on a piece of paper. The color absorbs into the dry or damp plaster.

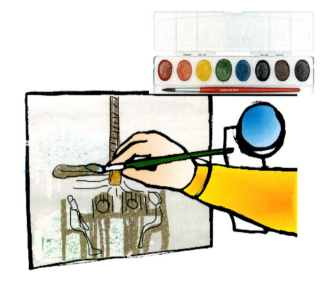

Lesson 5

Gothic Period

Limbourg

Paul, Jean, and Herman Limbourg, *LIHM burkh,* (? – early 1400's)

Our story starts with three brothers who painted for a very special Duke. Dukes were wealthy and had time and money to do whatever they pleased. The Duke of Berry liked to collect objects from foreign lands, including live animals. His collection of animals was much like a zoo is today. Have you visited a zoo? Have you drawn pictures of the animals there? The Duke gave the three brothers the job of painting what they saw in and around his castles.

Three brothers entered the Duke of Berry's castle gates. Paul, Jean, and Herman had been to the Duke's castle before, so the ostriches and camels, which had seemed so strange on their first visit, were welcome sights. Dogs eagerly greeted them with lapping tongues. Servants and guards greeted the brothers too, for everyone at the castle knew of their coming. The brothers were illuminators, painters of books and manuscripts, and the Duke had called for their services again.

As they entered the castle, they saw the Duke's treasures. Each room was decorated (Pioch). Tapestries, paintings, jewels, trinkets, and books lined the walls and floors. The Duke did not leave the brothers waiting long, for he was very excited about his new project.

Jean of Berry liked to have his picture portrayed in paintings by numerous artists, including the three Limbourg brothers.

"I want a Book of Hours, decorated so finely that a man must use a magnified lens to see the detail," announced the Duke. He continued, "Its colors must be like jewels, so bright that it takes a man's breath away. Let its pages show the splendor of my land!"

The brothers eagerly went to work. Paul talked to traders to obtain the expensive blue semi-precious stone, lapis lazuli, from the Middle East. He crushed the blue stones to make a fine powder. Adding liquids to the powder, he made brilliant blue paint that they would need for the paintings within the book.

Jean visited the local alchemist's shop to obtain the yellow lead compound he needed. The alchemist mixed elements in perfect amounts to make a new substance. At his workshop, Jean mixed the yellow lumps with crushed flowers to make a green color that sparkled like new leaves after a spring shower (Pioch).

Herman made brushes from the tail hairs of a squirrel. Each thin hair came to a fine point to create the tiny details that the Duke had asked for (Saitzyk 50). He carefully chose the hairs and tied them together to make brushes of different sizes.

With liquid paints, fine brushes, and the help of a magnified lens, the brothers painted each picture. The Book of Hours took the brothers several years to finish.

Because the Limbourg brothers painted the Duke of Berry's life and his surroundings during each month of the year (Owen), it gives us a picture into what life was like in the 1400's.

What is a Book of Hours?
Many men of royal birth owned a Book of Hours. Artists made the books by hand. They wrote each word by hand. A Book of Hours usually included inspiring words for each hour of the day. It also included prayers, the calendar, psalms, and masses for certain holy days. Each page was decorated with beautiful paintings.

Project 5: Papier-Mâché

> GROUP #4 MODELING
> - Instant **papier-mâché**
> - Tempera paint (Group #1)
> - Brush (Group #1)
> - Water container, paper towels

STUDENT GALLERY

"Tiger" was made by Olivia (age 7).

Before doing this project you may want to take a trip to the zoo, watch a wildlife video, look at animals in a book, or study your own pet. Answer these questions about the animal you've chosen. What shape is its body? What shape is its head? What kind of tail does it have? What kind of legs does it have and how many? Model the shape of the animal with instant papier-mâché.

Mix about a cup of papier-mâché with a small amount of warm water as stated on the package directions. It will look dry, but as you knead it, it will become the consistency of heavy dough.

1. When the mixture is stiff, roll it into a ball to form a body. Work on a piece of cardboard or paper to keep the table surface clean.

2. Make an animal by squeezing out a head, some legs and other parts from the body. Form the parts and the body until the animal looks the way you want it to. When finished, smooth the surface with your fingers. Allow the animal to dry completely. This will take a few days depending on the size of it.

3. When your animal is dry, paint it with tempera paint.

19

Lesson 6

August (Departure for the Falcon Hunt) by the Limbourg Brothers

This painting is part of a calendar used by the Duke of Berry. It shows the departure of the duke and his guests for a falcon hunt. This event is a perfect way to show the fine clothing and parade of decorated horses that accompany such an outing. The brothers gave special attention to the landscape. Landscape is the land and what is on it including trees, hills, and in this picture, the Duke's castle, the Chateau d'Etampes. As they often did, the brothers have included peasants in their painting. On this hot August day, some peasants take a dip in the ponds to cool off while others bring in the harvest.

Name some of the objects you see in the landscape.

How many dogs are in this painting?

Where are the falcons? (birds in people's hands)

What colors are the horses?

Can you find the man below in the painting? Here you can see the fine detail in the falcons and clothing.

Limbourg Brothers, *August (Departure for the Falcon Hunt)*, Calendar miniature from the Tres Riches Heures du Duc de Berry, 1416. Photo: R.G. Ojeda. Photo Credit: Réunion des Musées Nationaux / Art Resource, NY

Project 6: Calendar Page

> **GROUP #1 PAINTING**
> - Watercolor paint set
> - Watercolor paper, water can
> - Round brush, paper towel

STUDENT GALLERY

Leigh (age 7) shows her back yard in this painting created for the month of October.

The Duke of Berry lived in several magnificent castles. Many people lived and worked in his castles and on his land. The Limbourgh brothers included those people and their activities in their calendar paintings. Make a calendar picture using pencil and watercolors. Show the place where you live. Notice what is around your home and what it looks like during this month. You may want to make a copy of the calendar on the grid below and attach it to your picture. Write or draw on the calendar squares special dates and occasions.

Calendar Page for the Month of _____

Sunday	Monday	Tuesday	Wednesday	Thursday	Friday	Saturday

Lesson 7

Gothic Period

Van Eyck

Jan Van Eyck,
yahn van EYEK, (~1380–1441)

Have you played the game "I Spy"? One person chooses an object and says, "I spy with my little eye something…" then you say a word to describe the object. The other person guesses what the object might be. This game and many others like it require that you look carefully at the world. We know that Jan Van Eyck enjoyed putting objects into his paintings that could only be discovered by looking closely.

Young Jan loved playing visual games, especially those that required a sharp eye. He was always first to spot a bird twittering in a tree or the tracks of a deer across a path.

"I spy, with my eye, something red, and it's neither your coat nor cap," called out his friend.

Jan knew his friend thought himself quite clever, for red was a rare color in the early spring landscape and his friend had surely thought this would make the object more difficult to find. Jan knew his friend's mistake, for a red object would stand out against the green landscape. He eyed the landscape carefully. He listened. Then a slight flutter of wings caught his attention. "The robin!" he said. His friend slumped in defeat. "Look!" Jan said, for something else had caught his keen eyes. Jan pointed to tracks along the rock's edge. He told the story of the tracks while his friend listened.

"Jan," said his friend, "You should become a story teller with your talents."

"I will tell stories, but not with words. I will tell my stories with pictures," said Jan. "Then I can tell them in color!" Jan Van Eyck's quick use of eyes and ears, and his ability to captivate people's attention with a good story, allowed him to work for the Duke of Burgundy. He traveled to Spain and Portugal as a diplomat, while painting for wealthy and powerful men (Payne 32). Jan discovered stunning effects with oil paints, applying layers of thin glazes to produce shimmering results. Egg tempera, used in the past, was dull like flat paint, but oils made colors actually shine! Van Eyck used the smooth, glowing paint to show "the sheen of jewels, the glow of flesh, and the texture of cloth" (Filan 38). 15th century Europeans used expensive clothing to show their place in society. Laws were made to prohibit those of lesser nobility from wearing certain furs and fabrics. Those who could legally wear fine clothing wanted it seen, and a painter who could paint the textures convincingly was highly valued. Van Eyck painted many of the first portraits Europeans had seen in oil paint.

Jan Van Eyck never put away his interest in seeing. He wanted people to stare at his paintings long enough to discover hidden objects and all the fine details of fabric and fur.

Project 7: Watercolor Wash Painting

> GROUP #1 PAINTING
> - Watercolor paint set
> - Watercolor paper
> - Round brush, water container, paper towels
> - Masking tape

STUDENT GALLERY

This picture is by Cassandra (age 8).

Take a trip outdoors with a friend and play *I spy*. Then paint a picture of some things you saw. You can paint the sky using a watercolor wash. Follow the directions below.

Tape the edges of the watercolor paper to a table or flat surface to prevent the paper from curling when it gets wet. Soften the watercolor paints by placing a few drops of water into each color.

Dip a large brush into water. Brush back and forth across the top half of the paper, until a smooth layer of water covers it.

Then, dip the brush in the blue paint. Brush the color back and forth over the wet surface until it appears smooth. This smooth surface is called a wash. Let it dry.

Paint in the details of your picture. Remember to rinse out one color before putting the brush into another color!

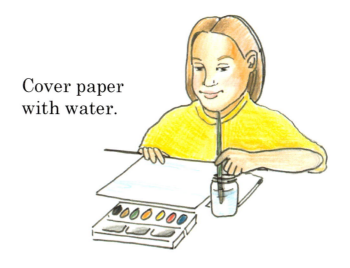

Cover paper with water.

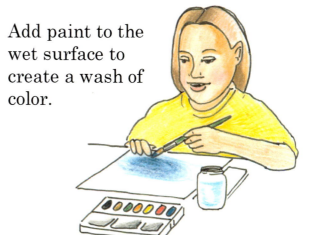

Add paint to the wet surface to create a wash of color.

Lesson 8

Jean Arnolfini and His Wife by Van Eyck

This is a wedding picture filled with Christian symbols. In this painting by Van Eyck, an Italian storeowner and his bride stand without shoes. It is a symbol that their marriage is holy just as Mosses removed his shoes when he stood on holy ground on Mount Sinai. They are dressed in their finest clothing. Mr. Arnolfini wears a fur-lined cloak. His wife wears a dress, which expands out in the front (the latest fashion of the time). Only one candle glows in the chandelier. It is a symbol for the presence of Jesus, described as "light" in the scriptures. The dog is a symbol for the couple's loyalty to each other, just as dogs are loyal to people.

Jan Van Eyck, *The Marriage of Giovanni Arnolfini and Giovanna Cerami*, 1434. Photo Credit: Dover Publications Inc.

Where are the two pairs of shoes in this painting? (Front left and center back)

How is this picture, painted nearly 600 years ago, different from a wedding photo you might see today? (colors of clothing, location, etc.)

What pieces of furniture do you see in this room? Beds with lots of fabric were a sign of great wealth and people of this time displayed them in main rooms, so the newly wedded couple is not standing in a bedroom as you might have guessed.

Project 8: Layering Oil Pastels

GROUP #2 DRAWING
- Oil pastels
- Drawing paper

Zeth (age 9) made this landscape drawing while sitting on the lawn.

Jan Van Eyck looked carefully at the world around him. Your world, like his, is filled with people and places to see. Go outdoors. Look at all that surrounds you. No one sees and understands the world as you see and understand it because no one has your eyes. Choose something in your world to draw. Draw in color with oil pastels.

Put pressure on the sticks of color so that you apply it thickly to drawing paper.

Layer one color over another so that they mix. For example, you might use dark blue, light blue, and white all within the sky or you might see orange, yellow, and red in fall trees.

White pastel does not show up on white paper, but it can be mixed with other colors, to make them lighter, as seen in this blue area.

25

Renaissance Period

Leonardo Da Vinci

Leonardo da Vinci, *duh VIHN chee,* (1452 – 1519)

Leonardo da Vinci was curious from birth and stayed that way his whole life. His curiosity drove him to look at and understand the world and how things work. Have you ever looked at something in nature and discovered something about it that you didn't know? What was it? Like Leonardo, you have a curious mind. You may be just as famous one day.

Piero da Vinci handed Leonardo's drawings to the great Florentine master, Andrea Verrocchio, in order to get an opinion on his son's talent. "Leonardo is always off on his own pursuits, but I think you'll find he is highly interested in learning the art of painting. He is always looking, always thinking, always aware of the possibilities," his father spoke proudly.

"Verrocchio was amazed when he saw Leonardo's extraordinary beginnings, and he urged Ser Piero to make Leonardo study art. Piero arranged for Leonardo to go to Andrea's (Verrocchio's) workshop, something Leonardo did very willingly" (Vasari 285).

At Verrocchio's shop Leonardo carefully studied his craft by drawing from life. One day his father brought him a roughly carved shield and asked him to paint a picture on it. Leonardo gave the shield to a turner who made it smoother and more even. He decided to make an image that would terrify anyone who saw it and turn them to stone as the head of Medusa is said to have done. Leonardo searched the countryside for strange creatures. Into his room he brought "crawling reptiles, green lizards, crickets, snakes, butterflies, locusts, bats, and other strange species of this kind, and by adapting various parts of this multitude, he created a most horrible and frightening monster emerging from a dark and broken rock, spewing forth poison from its open mouth, fire from its eyes, and smoke from its nostrils so strangely that it seemed a monstrous and dreadful thing indeed" (Vasari 288).

He studied the animals and insects so carefully and painted them with such attention to detail that he did not notice the awful smell of them. When Ser Piero came to pick up the finished shield, Leonardo played a trick on him. He set the shield on his easel so that it would be the correct height of the monster. Then he closed the curtains so that it was seen in a dim light. His father, not expecting a trick, entered the room and was immediately aware of the awful smell. Then he saw a horrible beast! He gasped and turned to leave. Leonardo laughed and said, "Take it away, for this was the intended effect" (Vasari 289). Ser Piero laughed too. He thought the work was fabulous and sold it for a large sum of money. Everyone loved Leonardo da Vinci. He had incredible talent, but he also had a sense of humor and curiosity that people enjoyed.

Leonardo da Vinci stayed curious during his entire lifetime. He studied the human body, stars, planets, plants, and the earth. He designed inventions and drew plans for mills, canals, and building structures. He used paint in new ways that marked the change from the Gothic artists to the Renaissance artists.

What is the Renaissance?

The Renaissance was a period when artists, architects, and intellectuals rediscovered the knowledge of ancient Greece and Rome. These men made fantastic advances in painting, building, and scientific knowledge, yet without the financial support of the Medici family, it would not have happened. Italian cities in the 1400's were each ruled by one family and the wealthiest was the Medici family of Florence. In order to impress and generate support, they spent money to have churches, public buildings, monuments, and art made.

Cosimo de' Medici is shown on the right, after a painting by artist, Pontormo. His grandson, Lorenzo de' Medici is shown on the left after a statue by artist, Verrocchio, Leonardo's teacher. These Medici men encouraged artists and builders to experiment and gave them opportunities to focus entirely on their work, without worry about where they would live or what they would eat. It is because of the Medici family's support, that we know the names of the great Renaissance artists, like Leonardo, architects like Brunelleschi, and sculptors like Michelangelo.

Project 9: Wash

GROUP #1 PAINTING
- Watercolor paint set
- Watercolor paper
- Brush
- Water container
- Paper towel
- pencil

STUDENT GALLERY

This self-portrait is by Marty (age 9).

Leonardo was interested in the proportions of the human face and body. Proportion is the measurement of how the parts fit together. When you look at a portrait by Leonardo, remember that people had never seen a photograph. They were amazed at the perfection of it. Leonardo blended the paint so that no brush marks were seen. The skin is perfectly smooth and each strand of hair was painted in detail. People wanting to have a likeness of themselves found that Leonardo could paint portraits to look more real than they had ever seen before.

To make colors look smooth we will water down the colors in the tray and apply a wash to the paper. A wash is a layer of water that is put over the paper. First, add water to an area in the mixing tray. Do all your color mixing in the tray, not in the colors. For dark skin, we added brown and red to the water. For light skin, we added orange and yellow to the water.

Draw a face with pencil. Brush water over the entire face that you have drawn on the paper. Then brush the mixed color into the water wash. The color will blend and you will see smooth transitions as you continue to work.

Allow the wash area to dry, and then add the details of eyes, mouth, and other parts.

The tray is the color mixing area!

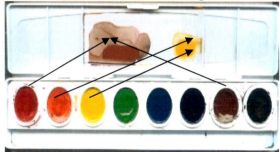

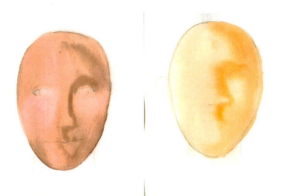

Lesson 10

Mona Lisa by Leonardo Da Vinci

Some say that *Mona Lisa* is the most famous painting of all time. You may wonder why. A look at other paintings from this period will give you a clue. People of nobility hired artists to paint their portraits. As one might suspect, kings, queens, and rich merchants tended to be spoiled and very demanding, so artists painted many portraits with sour or dull expressions. In this portrait, we see something different. Leonardo paints this person with expression. People wonder if she was enjoying some amusing story told by Leonardo. Whatever the reason for the smile, Leonardo captured it in his painting and people have been amazed by it ever since. He must have loved it too. It was the one painting he would not part with for his entire life.

Leonardo da Vinci, *Mona Lisa*, 1506. Photo Credit: Dover Publications Inc.

Here we see a picture of a woman, painted in the artist's studio. What does Leonardo put behind her?

Have you ever been in nature and felt a certain way: peaceful, calm, jumpy, or happy? How does the scenery in this painting make you feel?

Leonardo da Vinci is given credit for discovering the effect of atmospheric perspective. He noticed that particles in the air got in the way and made objects look bluer and more "smoky" as they went into the distance. This painting shows that effect.

Project 10: Textured Watercolor Painting

GROUP #1 PAINTING
- Watercolor paint set
- Watercolor paper
- Brush, water container, paper towel
- Plastic wrap

STUDENT GALLERY

Emilio (age 9) made this student work.

When artists paint portraits, they often paint the head, neck, and shoulders. This makes people look cut in half. Leonardo da Vinci had a new idea and included the arms and hands in his portrait called, "Mona Lisa." By including hands, we follow a path with our eyes that goes from the face to the hands and then back to the face. This makes the picture more pleasant to look at. Many people talk about her curious smile, but it is the hands that make this picture so pleasant. You can draw a portrait of yourself or someone you know that includes the arms and hands. Use watercolor and the technique shown for adding texture to the background.

Paint a portrait. Use watercolors as shown on page nine to paint the face, arms, and hands. Allow those areas to dry.

Apply the watercolor wash to the background in whatever color you desire, as shown on page twenty-three. While still wet, place wrinkled plastic wrap on the papers surface. Press it down. Leave it in place until it is dry. When dry, lift the plastic wrap from the painting. This creates an interesting texture on the surface of the painting.

Plastic wrap is placed over the wet background and allowed to dry.

30

Lesson 11

Renaissance Period

Michelangelo

Michelangelo Buonarroti, *MY KUHL an juh LOH,* (1475-1564)

Some people dream of mighty men and some become them. Michelangelo did both. He did not know, as a child, that he would create such powerful art that people would still talk about him 600 years later. What do you imagine yourself becoming when you grow up?

    As young Michelangelo sat before his studies, the characters seemed to rise forcefully from the pages. Great heroes like David who slew a mighty Philistine and powerful leaders like Brutus from ancient Rome grew huge in his mind. Michelangelo imagined what grand men they must be. He knew much about them, for he was from a respected Florence family and they learned about both theology (the study of God) and the cultures of ancient Greece and Rome. Both were important parts of a Renaissance education (Molho 233).

    Michelangelo must have felt that he too held some of their power because at the age of twelve he left his classical education to become an apprentice to the most popular painter in Florence, Domenico Ghirlandajo (*geer lahn DAH yoh*). Soon Lorenzo de Medici visited Ghirlandajo and told him of his love for the arts and his wish to take promising young students and have them trained in the medium of sculpture at his garden. Michelangelo was chosen. Before he'd been trained, he took a chisel in hand and began to carve a copy of an old and wrinkled faun statue that sat in Lorenzo's garden. Lorenzo was impressed with the copy because Michelangelo had made the laughing mouth open to show the tongue and teeth, but Lorenzo teased him by saying that no old man has all of his teeth. So, wanting to please him, Michelangelo chipped out a tooth. Lorenzo got such pleasure from this encounter that he took Michelangelo in as his own son to live with him and lavished all his wealth on him during his training in stone. With stone, Michelangelo could create the massive figures that always lingered in his mind. He could see what figure lay in the large marble slab. He cut the stone away with his chisel, until a figure emerged from the marble.

    As an adult, Michelangelo devoted all his time to large projects. His sculptures in marble show strong figures made larger than life.

Michelangelo's figures in both marble and paint show muscular men and women. Perhaps they are the same strong images that formed in Michelangelo's young mind as he read their stories.

Project 11: Carving

GROUP #4 CARVING
- Apple with no bruises
- Lemon juice and salt
- Plastic knife and peeler
- Construction paper (Group #5)
- Scissors (Group #5)
- Elmer's Glue-All

Michelangelo knew that he was a gifted sculptor. Carving into marble was his greatest enjoyment as an artist. He chipped away at a marble block until a figure emerged. You can cut away at an apple to carve a face.

STUDENT GALLERY

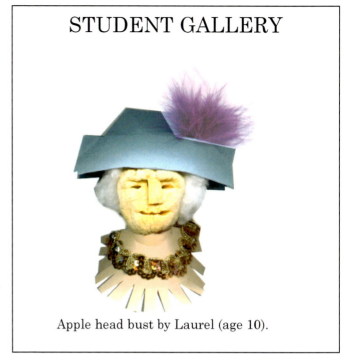

Apple head bust by Laurel (age 10).

1.

2.

3.

1. Peel an apple that is firm and has no bruises. With a plastic knife, make three cuts for the nose.
2. Remove wedges of the apple by cutting towards the cut lines of the nose. Be careful not to cut off the nose.
3. Cut slits for the eyes. Cut a slit for the mouth. Soak the apple for 20 minutes in enough water to cover the apple. Add 2 tablespoons of salt and 2 tablespoons of lemon juice to the water.
4. Place the carved apple head onto a paper cup to dry. Drying may take several weeks. The apple is ready when spongy.
5. Form a tube by gluing a rectangular strip together at the ends. Glue the dried apple onto it.
6. Research clothing of the Renaissance period. Hats and costumes were elaborate. Dress your apple head with cut out paper hats and collars. Hair can be made of cotton balls or other materials. Attach pieces to the apple with Elmer's Glue-All.

4.

This is how the apple will look after one day.

5.

The apple will be much smaller in two weeks.

Lesson 12

Delphic Sibyl by Michelangelo

Michelangelo, *Delphic Sibyl*, c. 1506-09.
Photo Credit: Dover Publications Inc.

In 1508, Michelangelo was commanded by the Pope to paint the ceiling of the Sistine Chapel. After much arguing, because he was having a good time sculpting and did not care to interrupt the work, he climbed the scaffolding and began a difficult job that would take four years to complete. Nine sections of the ceiling show pictures telling the major stories of Genesis, including the creation, the fall of Adam and Eve, and Noah and the flood. They are painted in bright color on plaster. Michelangelo and his assistants transferred his original pictures to the ceiling by attaching paper drawings to the ceiling and then scratching over the lines and marking into plaster while it is damp. Then Michelangelo applied the paint.

This picture of the Greek sibyl, sibyl meaning prophetess, shows the interest in Greek literature that educated men had during the Renaissance. Michelangelo included Greek icons as well as the ancient Hebrew stories within his ceiling paintings. He draws the sibyl with the strong arms of a man. His male figures were even more muscular. Remember Michelangelo for his strong figures, which show the power and force of his own personality.

Prophetesses were historically acknowledged to speak the words of the Hebrew God or Greek gods. What does Michelangelo place in her hands to show that she has knowledge? (a scroll)

33

Project 12: Fresco

GROUP #1 PAINTING
- Spackling paste
- Chipboard or cardboard
- Watercolor set
- Round brush

Isaac (age 6) made this work. A mighty man sits in the right corner. He looks out a doorway from inside his home.

Michelangelo's work on the Sistine Chapel was especially difficult because it was painted on the ceiling. He had to use a wooden platform and paint on his back while holding his hand above his head. Paint splashed onto his face and body as he looked up to work. It was very messy. A fresco must be painted quickly before the plaster dries, so he did this difficult work at a fast, steady pace throughout the entire day. You will have more success if you work in the opposite way, with the plaster surface below your head. Draw a strong person, a hero, or a leader you know.

Apply a thin layer of Spackle (available at the hardware store) over a piece of cardboard with a putty knife or small piece of cardboard with a straight edge. Once the spackle is dry or just damp, make grooves into the spackle with a pointed stick or pencil to draw your picture.

Prepare the watercolor paints by adding a few drops of water to each color.

Fill in the lines that you made, painting with watercolors just as you do on paper. The color absorbs into the plaster.

34

Renaissance Period   **Lesson 13**

Raphael

Raffaello Sanzio,
RA fih uhl, (1483–1520)

Raphael was schooled at home by his father, rather than by the traditional ways of his time. While young, Raphael observed his father's life as an artist. His father, Giovanni Santi, cared for his son dearly, and was his first teacher. It was customary to learn a skill by starting with the small parts of the task. Raphael performed these tasks as he worked beside his father. Have you worked beside your mother, father, or another adult to do or make something?

Raphael sat on the floor of his father's studio grinding the lumps of red mineral into a fine powder with a small mortar and pestle. This was the first step to making his father's paint. How he wanted to be finished, but if he quit too soon his father would look into the bowl and say that it must be crushed finer. As Raphael ground the powder, he dreamed of holding the paintbrush someday like his father. He looked up, longing to paint. The outlined face of the Duke of Urbino stared back at him from his father's painting. Raphael could feel the colors, forms, and lines that magically came together through his father's brush to become like the real person.

His father's voice broke the silence. "Good, Raphael. Now mix the binder into the fine pigment you've ground and you may paint from this bowl with the brush you tied yesterday." Tying the fine hairs around sticks of wood to make brushes, grinding the powder to make paint and sharpening leads for drawing were part of every young artist's training during the Renaissance. Raphael's training under his father's guidance was his first step to become an artist (Becherucci 10, 11).

At age eleven Raphael began studies with Perugino, who his father recognized as an important painter and one who would help his talented son thrive in the new ideas of the times (Zafran 142). Raphael was quick to pick up new techniques as they developed.

Raphael made many paintings of Mary and Jesus for churches. In them, we see his ability to paint people as though they were real, as though they were actually staring back, just as his father's portraits stared at him when he was young.

A young apprentice mixes oil and pigments (colors) with a stone slab and Muller. The artist's pallet shows most of the colors available during the Renaissance.

Where did Renaissance colors come from?

In Raphael's time, the colors came from natural things that colorists found in or on the earth. Paints were made from metals, leaves, animals, and minerals. Ink bags of cuttle fish were dried to make sepia (brown). Fermented, ripe berries of the buckthorn were crushed to make sap green. Mummies from Egypt were ground up to make mummy brown. Lead white was made by corroding lead plates with acid in clay pots and then burying them in manure piles to produce heat. A white substance formed and was then scrapped off and ground to a powder to make paint. Blacks were made from burnt peach pits or grapevines, burnt tusks of sea animals, and burnt oils that collected on lamps (Saitzyk 193). Colors were held together with binders such as oils extracted from sunflowers, linseed, or poppies. Beeswax was sometimes mixed in. Ingredients were mixed by hand. The artist used a stone Muller on a stone slab to mix oil and pigment. A thin layer of oil coated each particle, giving the pigment a glossy look. Many paint ingredients were dangerous and artists often became sick from using them, without knowing the cause. People no longer grind up mummies or use lead in paints. Today big machines crush and mix safer ingredients to make paint.

Project 13: Tempera Painting

> **GROUP #1 PAINTING**
> - Tempera paint
> - Watercolor paper
> - Flat brush

This winter tree was painted by Gavi (age 8).

Raphael used oil paints, which can be layered on top of each other and blended. You can use tempera. Follow the instructions below when using tempera paints. One color can be brushed on top of another once the first color is dry.

Set up the paints so that everything is within easy reach. Paint supplies should include the tempera paints, paper, paintbrush, paper towel, and a water container for rinsing the brush. A flat brush is good for getting the thick paint from the jar, mixing colors, and covering large areas of the paper.

Dip the brush into the paint jar. Apply paint directly to the paper. Do not dip up to the metal part of the brush.

To change colors:

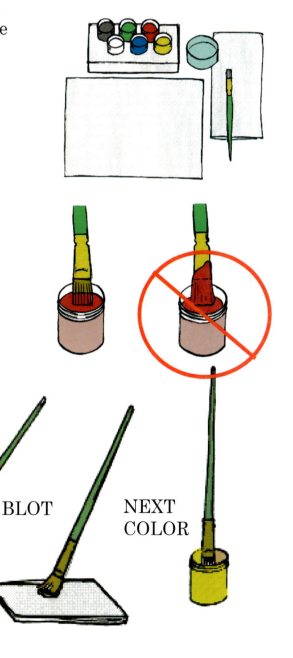

WASH WIPE BLOT NEXT COLOR

37

Lesson 14

Portrait of a Young Woman (Lady with a Unicorn) by Raphael

Raphael was friendly and liked people. This quality shows in his art. This painting shows the human qualities of tenderness and trust. The young girl's fingers gently play with the Unicorn's legs as it sits in her arms. It is an early work of Raphael's and shows an interest in medieval iconography. A young woman represents purity. It was a common idea that the wild unicorn could only be tamed by a young maiden. The unicorn would lie on her lap and fall asleep. Medieval and Renaissance literature and paintings made many references to unicorns and maidens. We can remember Raphael for the human quality of tenderness that his paintings show us.

Raphael Santi, *Portrait of a Young Woman (Lady with a Unicorn)*, 1505-06. Photo Credit: Dover Publications Inc.

How is this painting similar to *Mona Lisa* by Leonardo da Vinci? (See page 29)

How is it different from *Mona Lisa* by Leonardo da Vinci?

Unicorns have been shown in art as lion-like, goat-like, horse-like, or lamb-like creatures. What animals do you think Raphael was thinking about as he painted his small version of a unicorn?

Project 14: Blending Tempera Paint

> **GROUP #1 PAINTING**
> - Tempera paint
> - Watercolor paper
> - Flat brush
> - Water container, paper towel

Raphael practiced the *sfumato* style of painting, used in the Renaissance. This style uses soft edges. You can use soft edges when mixing colors.

Amber (age 8) painted this work.

Dark colors are stronger than light colors. They can easily overpower a lighter color. When mixing colors, always pick up a large amount of the light color first. Put it onto a paper plate. Then add a small dab of the darker color. Mix the colors together. Apply the mixed color to the picture.

To make a *sfumato* sky, follow these directions. Mix white with a small amount of blue. Apply the blue color across the top part of the paper.

Next, mix white with a small amount of red. Apply the pink mixture across the paper next to the sky blue.

While still wet, brush across both colors where they meet until they mix and the line is softened.

Next, mix white with a small amount of yellow. Apply the yellow mixture across the paper next to the pink. Soften the edge where the pink and yellow colors meet. Paint a picture on top of the sky.

Lesson 15

Renaissance Period

Anguissola

Sofonisba Anguissola (1532-1625)

What kind of job do you dream of having when you grow up? Anguissola may never have dreamed that she would travel to another country to work for a queen. That is just what she did, all because of her love for painting.

"Sofonisba wants to paint. Who will sit for Sofonisba now?" called her youngest sister.

"Let Sofonisba be her own model," called back another sister as she contemplated her next move on the chessboard.

Sofonisba Anguissola ran into the room. "Have you heard, my dear sisters? Father has written to the great Michelangelo to request a drawing by his own hand, that I might paint it!"

"You should practice even harder, if that be so," stated her sister, "so that your hand at painting won't ruin a fine sketch by the master artist."

Sofonisba laughed, for no teasing would ruin her good mood. "I shall practice, dear sister. I shall draw you as you are today, so that the world will remember the Anguissola sisters."

Sofonisba and her three sisters were born into a noble family in Italy. They all had artistic talent, but Sofonisba proved to be the most skillful. Noble families purchased her paintings. She studied painting for six years, then "was spotted by the Duke of Alba in Spain (Payne 69)." She moved to Spain and there her talent for painting portraits was rewarded when she became a court painter and lady-in-waiting to Queen Isabel of Spain.

Sofonisba Anguissola is one of the few well-known women artists of the sixteenth century. The support of her caring father and her own talent for painting portraits are the main reasons for her success and why we find her name in art books today.

Project 15: Tempera over Oil Pastels

GROUP #2 DRAWING
- Oil pastels
- Chipboard or heavy paper
- Brush, scratch tool
- Black tempera paint (Group #1)

STUDENT GALLERY

Caleb (age 8) outlined a tree in black, filled the spaces with color, and then applied black paint. Once it was dry, he scratched off the entire picture surface. The black textured surface looks beautiful over the bright colors!

Anguissola used dark and light colors in her paintings. The dark colors stand out against the light colors. You can use the bright colors of oil pastels and then surround them in black paint. The colors look brighter when surrounded by black, rather than the white of the paper.

1. Apply Pastel.

2. Apply Paint. Let Dry.

3. Scratch Paint Off.

Draw a picture using oil pastels. Fill in your shapes with solid colors. Add a bit of water to a spoonful of black tempera paint to make it thinner. Brush the black paint across the entire picture, even over the oil pastel. When the paint is the right consistency, it sticks to the white paper, but not completely to the oil pastel. Let the paint dry. Scratch some of the paint off the colored areas with a large nail, stick, or other pointed tool. Michaela (age 7) scraped off black paint to show the colors (above). In this picture, a deer hides behind a tree.

Lesson 16

A Game of Chess by Anguissola

In this painting, we see Anguissola's sisters playing chess. An older woman, their servant, watches. Anguissola had a talent for painting delicate things. Look at the many hands within the picture. They look graceful. The details in the clothing are carefully painted so that the patterns and decorations are clearly seen. She paints the leaves on the trees as carefully as the intricate pattern on the tablecloth. The landscape in the background, painted in blue colors, is typical of a Renaissance portrait painting. You have also seen this technique used in the *Mona Lisa*.

Sofonisba Anguissola (1532-1625)
A Game of Chess, involving the painter's three sisters and a servant. 1555. Canvas, 72 x 97 cm.
Location: Museum Narodowe, Poznan, Poland
Photo Credit: Erich Lessing / Art Resource, NY

Which sister looks like she is having the most fun?

Which sister looks confident?

Which sister is concentrating or thinking about her next move?

The table tilts toward us so that we can see the top. Why did the artist paint it this way?

Project 16: Dark Ground Drawing

GROUP #2 DRAWING
- Oil pastels
- Construction paper (Group #5)

Nathan (age 6) drew a picture of himself and his twin brother as they have fun in the rain.

Anguissola made the little girl stand out in the painting A *Game of Chess*. She did this by placing the girl's light face against a dark tree. Light colors stand out more when seen against dark colors. You can do this too. Oil pastels come in light and dark colors. Draw with oil pastels on colored paper. Make a picture of yourself with brothers, sisters, or friends.

Oil pastels are very soft, which makes them easy to use. Do not worry if the sticks break. Just peel back the paper and use up the entire stick. You can draw with the side of the stick too.

Do you see how the light colors stand out on darker paper in the picture above?

Lesson 17

Northern Renaissance

Durer

Albrecht Durer,
DYUR uhr, (1471-1528)

Have you ever taken a walk and noticed a rock, leaf, or small creature that was so interesting you had to stop and take a closer look? Artists notice the beauty of objects in our world. Albrecht Durer saw the beauty and uniqueness in a variety of small objects. This ability made him a great artist.

Albrecht followed his father's footsteps closely as they walked through the narrow Nuremberg streets. An evening chill made him glad his father's patrons were important men of the city so that his father could afford to give him a warm cloak to wear. Suddenly his father stopped and Albrecht bumped into him. The jolt knocked him backward to the ground.

His father looked down at him and laughed. "Look at the setting sun," he said. "It is as round and golden as the gold plates we made for the emperor."

Albrecht stood up beside his father. He stared at the sun in silence as a golden light spread over his cloak, the land, and the buildings of the city. Nature had a way of making his busy father become still. Albrecht remembered the stag beetle with a huge head and spiky mandibles that crawled across the studio floor that summer, during a painting lesson. His father stopped the lesson. They got on their hands and knees to study the beetle closely.

Albrecht's father taught him all he knew about goldsmithing, painting, and observing the world around him. By age thirteen Albrecht painted his first self-portrait. The following year he became an apprentice to his father. One year later, he was apprenticed to Michael Wolgemut. There he learned to make woodcut illustrations. Durer was the first artist to produce and sell his own art to the public.

Albrecht Durer, *Self-Portrait*, 1498.
Photo Credit: Dover Publications Inc.

Durer worked within the Renaissance period as Leonardo da Vinci, Michelangelo, and Anguissola did, but he worked in a country further north. All these artists made exciting discoveries during their lifetimes, but it was Durer's keen observation of detail that marked his greatness. He created finely detailed woodcuts.

Look at the print by Durer on page forty-eight. It was made with one of the first printing presses. Printing presses were used to make more than one copy of the same drawing. These copies are called prints. Artists carved a picture into a piece of wood. Ink was rolled over the carved wood, which was placed on a press (inked side up). Paper was placed over the inked carving and the artist slid them under the stamping mechanism of the press. The artist guided the handle down, bringing great force onto the inked woodcarving and paper. The handle was lifted to slide the work out from under the press. The inked drawing was seen on the paper. A print was made!

Did the printing press change art?

Before the invention of the printing press, a drawing with lines was the first step to a painting. Artist's line drawings were not considered finished art. The printing press allowed artists to draw pictures onto wooden slabs and then transfer the image to paper many times. These images could be inserted into books. Line drawings became finished works for books and later accepted as finished works of art. Paintings continued to be created, however prints gave artists another acceptable way to produce images. People who could not afford a painting were now able to purchase less expensive prints. Hand colored religious prints were popular at this time.

45

Introduction to Printmaking

This print was made using a process described on page 51.

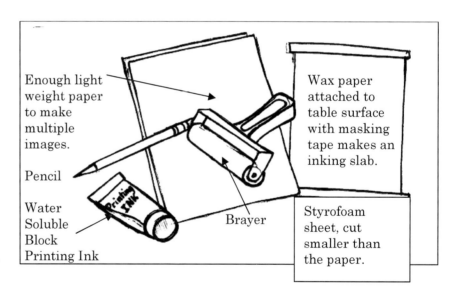

Printmaking is a very exciting medium for children. They love to transfer an image from one surface to another, seemingly by magic. Even if you have never made a print before, you can successfully guide students through this exciting process.

We use a surface covered in wax paper as an inking slab to make clean up easy. An inking slab is where ink is applied to the brayer and the plate. The brayer is a tool for rolling out the ink. A plate is sometimes used to make the first image. Wax paper, held down by masking tape, covers the table's surface during all steps of the process: inking the brayer, inking the plate (when needed), and transferring the image. When finished, lift the wax paper from the table surface and throw it away. Wax paper is a cheap and convenient method for the home and for classrooms.

Always use **water soluble** block printing inks. Instruct students to keep their hands clean, using only the brayer to touch the ink. Wash hands and the brayer with water to clean.

These are the tools you and your child need to make prints. The first types of prints will not use a Styrofoam sheet for the plate. In the first prints, your child will draw directly into the ink or make marks on the back side of a sheet of paper.

A variety of ink colors can be used. Several colors can be squeezed onto the wax paper and rolled together with a brayer to mix.

Go to the next page to find instructions for making a mono-print.

Project 17: Monoprint
(Drawing into the Ink)

> **GROUP #3 PRINTMAKING**
> - Brayer, and a pencil
> - Wax paper and masking tape
> - Printmaking ink
> - Drawing paper

STUDENT GALLERY

Allison (age 5) made this student work of a snowman in snow.

A monoprint is the simplest method for making a print. A plate is not used. The image is made directly onto the wax paper surface. Using this method only one print can be pulled.

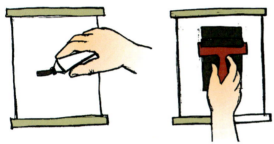

Your adult helper should prepare your space by placing a sheet of wax paper on the table and attaching it with masking tape. They should squeeze the water-soluble ink onto the wax paper. The amount of ink should be double to the amount of toothpaste used to fill a toothbrush.

With a brayer, you roll the ink over the surface until it evenly covers an area slightly larger than the width of the brayer. This will take some time.

Draw into the ink with any type of tool such as the eraser side of a pencil, a broad pen point, a plastic spoon, or a Popsicle stick. Take care not to tear through the wax paper.

Once your drawing in ink is finished, place a sheet of paper over it and rub the entire surface of the paper with the side of your fist. Pull the paper from the surface. The paper will show a reversed image of your drawing.

Tip: Keep your hands clean. This is not a finger-painting project. When hands do get ink on them, wash it off with water before it gets onto unwanted surfaces. Come back to the project with dry hands.

Lesson 18

The Flight into Egypt by Durer

Durer became a loyal supporter of Martin Luther, a German monk who started the Protestant movement in 1517. Because of Luther's teachings, Durer saw his Christian faith in a new light (Pioch). He saw God as the caring creator of nature. To him this truth meant that a simple object such as a beetle, rabbit, or plant was important to God and therefore important enough to draw. Durer brought his excellent skills and his appreciation for nature together in works that gained him great respect. Durer was praised for the way he used many different types of lines.

Can you find the child?

This shows Joseph, Mary, and baby Jesus fleeing to Egypt. What belongings do they take with them?

Can you find the angels?

Can you find a **donkey, cow, deer, bird, two lizards, and a rabbit** in this picture?

Albrecht Durer (1471-1528)
The Flight into Egypt. From the Marienleben (Life of Mary). 1511. Woodcut. (B.89)
Location: Bayerische Staatsbibliothek, Munich, Germany
Photo Credit: Foto Marburg / Art Resource, NY.

Project 18: Monoprint
(Drawing on the Back Side of the Paper)

> GROUP #3 PRINTMAKING
> - Brayer, and a pencil
> - Wax paper and masking tape
> - Printmaking ink
> - Drawing paper

Moriah (age 5) made this monoprint. She began with red and blue ink on the wax paper surface.

Durer was fascinated by the world. The very simplest things became objects worthy of drawing and painting. Think of the small things that seem interesting to you. In your next monoprint, draw something you find fascinating. You can make a monoprint in a different way than in the previous project. See the directions below.

Your adult helper should place a sheet of paper under the wax paper and tape the wax paper to the table surface with masking tape. The sheet of paper will be a guide for you so that you know where the edges of your final sheet will be. The wax paper is your inking slab (where you roll out the ink).

Roll ink onto the inking slab with a brayer in the same manner as you did in the first method. Take care not to exceed the size of the paper underneath as you roll out the ink.

Cover the inked area with a sheet of paper. Draw lines with a pencil on the top side of this sheet. Be careful not to rest your hand on the paper while drawing. When the drawing is finished, lift the paper. The print is on the back of your pencil drawing. You will see dark lines where you drew, with some imprint of ink on the areas in between the lines.

Lesson 19

Northern Renaissance

Bruegel

Pieter Bruegel the Elder,
PEE tuhr BROY guhl, (~1525 – 1569)

People may dress differently, speak a different language, or celebrate holidays in a different manner from your own family. How do you act around people who are different from you in some way? In Pieter Bruegel's day people separated themselves by the amount of money or possessions they owned. Rich families rarely mingled with the poor. However, Pieter Bruegel was different. He saw the poor and his paintings gave others greater understanding of the way that they lived, loved, worked, and played.

"Good Sir!" Pieter called to the peasant who skillfully skated past him on the frozen canal. "Let me use your skates so that I can enjoy the ice." Skating was a favorite past time of his people, yet Pieter Bruegel rarely had the time to do it. He was well educated as a child and study still took up most of his day. Those long hours of study had led him to Antwerp, Belgium, to study painting with two well-known artists. The sun soon set and Pieter returned the skates to the generous man. The man bowed with a humble smile to thank Pieter, for Pieter's fine clothing and manner told him that Pieter was a young city man and not one of the poor, like himself. Pieter returned the smile, for although he was from a wealthy family, he did not feel the need to look down on the poor the way many of his class did.

As Pieter walked back to his home, he thought about this kind and generous group of people. They struggled for meager things like food, warm homes, and safety yet they had time to play, time to dance, and time to enjoy the land they lived on and the people who were their neighbors. Perhaps, he thought, they have strength of character worth noting.

These peasants later became the subjects that Pieter Bruegel focused on in his paintings. He painted folk customs, scenes of their struggles, and scenes of their joys. His pictures encouraged later Flemish and Dutch painters to paint the customs of their own countries.

Project 19: Relief Print

> GROUP #3 PRINTMAKING
> - Brayer
> - Printmaking ink
> - Styrofoam sheets for printmaking
> - Wax paper and masking tape
> - Drawing paper (Group #2)

STUDENT GALLERY

Dakota (age 9) made this relief print of a duck.

In a relief print, the highest surface is inked and printed. Any indentions in the surface remain white. Use a flat piece of Styrofoam for your printing plate. This could be a Styrofoam plate, meat tray, or purchased sheets from art supply stores. Make sure the paper you print on is larger than the piece of Styrofoam plate. If you are using a 9x12 inch Styrofoam plate, cut it in half or quarters. Draw into the Styrofoam plate with a dull pencil, leaving deep grooves in the plate.

1. Ink is transferred from the wax surface to the brayer.

2. Ink is transferred from the brayer to the plate.

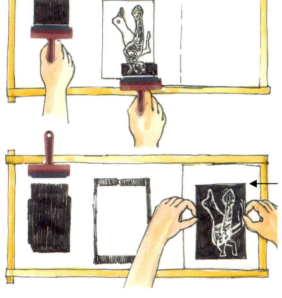

Move the plate from the second workspace and center in the third space, ink side up.

3. Ink is transferred from the plate to the paper.

Your adult helper should attach a long sheet of wax paper to a table surface with masking tape. Allow for three workspaces as shown. Place a sheet of paper the same size as your print paper under the wax paper, in the third work space, to use as a guide when placing the paper onto the plate in the final step.

Ink up the brayer on the first workspace. Ink should not be thick or glossy, but rolled until it obtains a matted sheen. Place your Styrofoam plate, drawing side up, in the second workspace. Roll the ink onto the Styrofoam plate using the brayer. Pick up more ink on the brayer by rolling over the ink surface in the first workspace. Next, place the inked Styrofoam plate face up in the center of the paper guide, which lies under the waxed paper.

Place a piece of paper over the Styrofoam plate and rub over the entire surface with the side of your fist. Lift the paper from the Styrofoam plate and let it dry.

The final image is reversed. You can ink up the same Styrofoam sheet again and make another copy of it using this method. Make many copies!

Lesson 20

Hunters in the Snow by Bruegel

Pieter Bruegel is often called "the Elder" meaning "older one." This is to set him apart from his two sons and their sons, who were also well known artists. Many of his descendants followed the elder Bruegel's example because he and his paintings were well liked during his lifetime and long after. This painting is one of six ordered by a wealthy Antwerp merchant to show seasons. The winter landscape shows hunters returning from a hunt with their dogs. Peasants cook. The background is full of activity. People ice skate and carry bundles. We can remember Pieter Bruegel the Elder for his view of peasant life, painted in such a pleasant manner that we often want to jump into the painting and join them in their activities.

Pieter Bruegel, *Hunters in the Snow*, 1565. Photo Credit: Dover Publications Inc.

How many hunters do you see? How many dogs traveled with the hunters?
Look at the way the row of trees carries you down into
the center of the painting. How many birds are found?
Why do you think people travel on the ice rather than through the snow to accomplish their business?

Project 20: Veggie Prints

> GROUP #1 PAINTING
> - Tempera paint
> - Light colored construction paper (Group #5)
> - Flat brush, water container, paper towel
> - Raw vegetables, paper plate

This picture of Zack and his twin brother was made by Zack (age 7). He used an onion, bell peppers, broccoli, a corncob, carrots, and celery to stamp his picture.

Bruegel painted scenes of the activities of people during their day. Think of a scene from your life or the lives of people you know. Paint it using stamping. Stamping is a form of making prints. You can stamp nearly anything onto paper if it has a flat surface that can be covered with paint and then pressed onto a piece of paper.

Vegetables make great stamps because they come in so many shapes and sizes. Choose different vegetables like celery, broccoli, carrots, radishes, or cabbage. Have an adult helper cut the vegetables so that they have flat surfaces. Place them on a paper plate.

Brush tempera paint onto the flat side of a vegetable. Stamp it onto a piece of construction paper. Experiment for a while to see what kinds of shapes each vegetable piece makes. Then, begin a picture on a new colored piece of paper. Broccoli spears make good trees. Bell peppers make great cloud shapes.

Return the painted vegetables to the paper plate to keep your work area clean. You can repaint vegetables to make more than one of the same shape.

You can paint objects into the picture with a brush too. The ground hogs in the picture at the right were painted with a brush.

53

Mannerist Period

Lesson 21

Parmigianino

Girolamo Francesco Maria Mazzola (1503-1540)

called Parmigianino

Do you ever think of new ways to do things? Parmigianino, a young boy from Parma, was always experimenting with the way art was made. He often exaggerated portions of his figures and that was highly unusual in his time. Sometimes people did not like his experimentation, but that did not stop Parmigianino.

Young Girolamo, who would later be called Parmigianino, studied the convex mirror with fascination. The barber's mirror had been left in his Uncle's study. His Uncle raised him after his father's early death and trained Parmigianino to be an artist. Parmigianino was sure of his skills as a painter, and practiced all the rules of realistic form passed down by the famous masters of the Renaissance. A thought formed in his mind. What would happen if he painted what he saw in the convex mirror? He held it close to his face, then far away. He angled it one way and then another. He noticed how the window behind him curved and how his hand appeared very large and strange. To make the image even stronger he hired a woodworker to carve a piece of wood to the exact dimensions of the mirror to make it convex too.

Self-Portrait in a Convex Mirror, 1524 by Parmigianino
Photo Credit: Dover Publications Inc.

Then he painted on the carved wood. The painting, created at age twenty-one, shocked Renaissance Italy. Parmigianino took it to Rome and was instantly given commissions to create other artworks. He went on to experiment with exaggerated forms. Without knowing it, his curiosity had led his art in new directions.

Parmigianino is remembered for making art that brought new drama, distortion, and exaggeration to the orderly reality created by Renaissance painters. These are the characteristics of the Mannerist painters.

Project 21: Watercolor Lift

GROUP #1 PAINTING
- Watercolor set
- Watercolor paper
- Round brush
- Paper towel

Annie Marie (age 9) made this student work showing a sky full of angels and clouds.

Parmigianino painted the self-portrait by looking at himself in a distorted mirror. Later he would use more imagination and distort the length of the human body in other ways. Use your imagination and paint figures with a blue background. Follow the instructions below to make a blue sky with fluffy clouds for your background.

With masking tape, attach a piece of watercolor paper to a smooth surface to prevent excessive wrinkling. Draw figures or objects on the paper.

Next, paint the sky around them by dipping a watercolor brush in water and covering the sky area with a wash of water. Dip the brush into blue paint and spread the color back and forth over the watery surface to get a smooth area of blue. While the paint is still wet, wrinkle a paper towel and dab it onto part of the blue area. It lifts the color off the paper to make it look like a cloud. Make as many clouds as you want. You can paint the sky is several different sections.

Let the wash dry. Then paint the figures or objects that you drew earlier.

Lesson 22

The Conversion of Paul by Parmigianino

Parmigianino, *The Conversion of Paul*, c. 1530.
Photo Credit: Dover Publications Inc.

    The Mannerists were known for dramatic light effects and distortion of the figures within their paintings. They wanted to stir the emotions through exaggeration. The theme Parmigianino has chosen to paint is one of the most dramatic within the Bible, the conversion of Paul. Paul persecuted Christians and was knocked off his horse, and blinded for a time in order for God to get his attention. The voice of God is implied in the clouds in the upper left corner. The beam of light looks unnatural and foreboding.

Which part of the horse looks a bit too small?
Does the neck look too long?
This distortion of the head and neck makes the horse look huge and adds to the drama of the story.

Project 22: Blocking Out

> GROUP #1 PAINTING
> - Watercolor paint set
> - Watercolor paper
> - Masking tape
> - Scissors
> - Round brush

STUDENT GALLERY

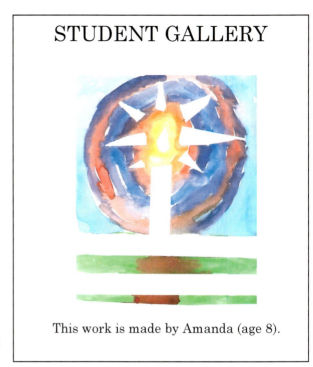

This work is made by Amanda (age 8).

Look again at *The Conversion of Paul* by Parmigianino. To make the light seem bright, he has painted a dark sky and dark shadows on the ground beneath Paul. You can create the same dramatic effect using light and dark contrast. Block out light areas of your painting then paint dark colors around them.

Cut masking tape and apply it lightly to a sheet of watercolor paper so that it blocks off the white paper.

Paint over the masking tape as you brush on the colors.

Let the painting dry. Carefully pull off the masking tape to reveal the white areas. You may add some color inside the white areas, as we did in the candle flame, to complete the picture.

1. Cut shapes from masking tape and apply them to the paper.

2. Brush paint over the paper and the tape.

3. Remove tape once the picture is dry.

Baroque Period Lesson 23

Rembrandt
Rembrandt van Rijn, *REHM brandt,* (1606 –1669)

Have you ever played dress up in some unusual or fancy clothes? Rembrandt collected dress-up items to dress models for his paintings. He lived in a time when men and women's costumes were very extravagant.

Rembrandt believed it truly was the "golden age of Holland." He prepared for another day in his artist's studio, surrounded by the treasures he had purchased. He thought back to his father, the owner of a large and busy windmill. With that mill, his father had ground grain into powder to produce simple products like bread. Rembrandt would not live simply. With his training, he ground precious minerals instead of the grain. The powder became fine liquid paint. With the paint, he created great works of art. How far he had come from his humble beginnings in Leiden!

Rembrandt lived in Amsterdam, the biggest port in Europe. There one could find the finest spices and rare art objects. Merchants and businessmen became wealthy quickly and with their money, they commissioned paintings of themselves and their families from Rembrandt. With money earned from painting, he bought a large, expensive house. He also purchased a collection of rich fabrics, jewelry, weapons, sculptures, and art from great Italian masters to be used in his paintings.

Rembrandt Van Rijn, *Self-Portrait*, 1640. Credit: Dover Publications Inc.

In Amsterdam, men could print books without gaining the king's approval first. They could express their own ideas, even if they were contrary to the king's ideas. So, the greatest artists, teachers, thinkers, and writers lived there. Rembrandt kept company with these intellectual men. Books required illustrations, and Rembrandt drew pictures onto metal plates to be printed in the books.

Rembrandt's dark portraits are some of the most famous portraits in the world. He made many self-portraits.

Project 23: Stamp Printing

Rembrandt bought expensive fabrics and clothing from far away lands. The merchandise came to Amsterdam by ships that had sailed around the world. In east Africa a special cloth is made using solid bright fabric that is stamped with patterns. You can find out more about Adinkra cloth by searching the web or looking for information at your local library.

> GROUP #1 PAINTING
> - Black tempera paint
> - Construction paper or piece of bright cloth
> - Craft Foam
> - Scissors, glue
> - Cardboard pieces
> - Flat brush

STUDENT GALLERY

This work was created by Laurel (age 6) and her mother.

THE STAMP

To make a stamp, cut a piece of cardboard and a piece of foam to the same size. Two inches by two inches works well.

Draw a stamp design onto the foam with a ballpoint pen or pencil. Keep the design simple.

Cut out the design. The foam cuts easily. Glue the foam to the cardboard base. Let it dry.

STAMPING THE CLOTH

With a flat brush, apply a coat of paint to the foam. Immediately turn the stamp upside down and press it onto a colored piece of construction paper or cloth. Lift the stamp to see the design.

Apply another coat of paint to the foam and stamp in a different area of the paper or cloth. You can stamp repeatedly!

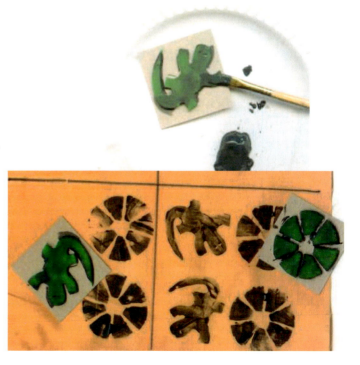

Lesson 24

Abraham Speaking with Isaac by Rembrandt

This is one of Rembrandt's printed scenes from the book of Genesis. In this scene, we see Abraham speak to his son, Isaac, explaining that God will provide the ram for the sacrifice about which Isaac has asked. Abraham's finger points toward the heavens as he explains. Isaac listens with interest while his eyes fix on his father. Here, as in his other works, Rembrandt captures the emotion of the characters through gesture and expression.

This work of art is an etching. Using acid, lines are etched into the metal. Once finished, the lines are filled with ink and transferred to paper. Look closely at the lines within the print.

Do you see straight lines? Where?

Do you see crossed lines? Where?

Do you see squiggly lines? What is described using squiggly lines?

Do you see lines for shading?

Can you find the artist's signature?

Rembrandt Harmensz van Rijn (1606-1669)
Abraham speaking with Isaac. 1645. Etching.
Photo Credit: Foto Marburg / Art Resource, NY

Project 24: Relief Print Card

Words and pictures go together. Rembrandt made pictures for books. You can make pictures for a card. To make a card, fold a piece of paper in half. Cut a Styrofoam plate smaller than the folded card. Follow the process for creating a relief print.

Make a drawing on a Styrofoam plate while your adult helper sets up the wax paper workspaces as shown on page 51.

Roll out the printmaking ink and transfer it from the wax paper to the brayer.

Roll the inked brayer onto the Styrofoam plate. Move the plate to a clean piece of wax paper.

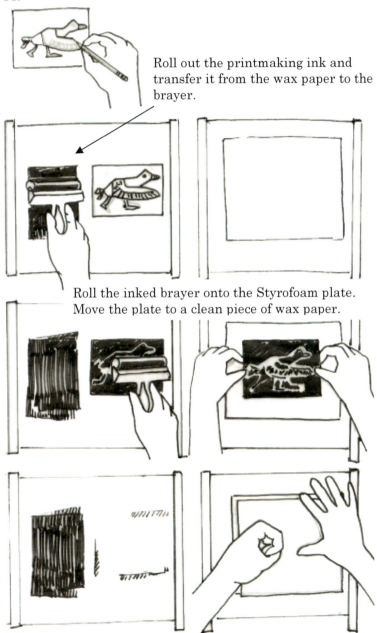

Open the folded card. Lay the card onto the inked plate in the area you want the print to appear. Rub it firmly with the side of your fist until the ink is transferred to the card. Lift the card and allow it to dry.

STUDENT GALLERY

Works by Michael (age 8) and Lindsey (age 9).

GROUP #3 PRINTMAKING
- Brayer
- Printmaking ink
- Styrofoam sheets for printmaking
- Wax paper and masking tape
- Pencil
- Drawing paper
- Construction paper

You may want to write a note in your card and send it to a friend! Michael made the card on top. The card below it, by Lindsey, was made on two sheets. Black ink on white paper was used for the picture. Gold ink on black paper was used for the frame. One Styrofoam sheet was used for the picture and another was used for the frame.

Lesson 25

Baroque Period

Vermeer Johannes Vermeer,
Yahn vur MEER, (1632-1675)

Is there a special place where you like to spend your time? Where is it? What do you do there? Jan Vermeer's father owned an inn that was just such a place for Jan. Most of his paintings are of the people and rooms in the inn his father purchased in Delft.

Young Jan sat up in his bed and watched as the pink rays of the sun flowed into the room from the window. Warmth spread over him like an extra blanket thrown across his shoulders. He was secure in his father's large inn, safe in the walled-in city of Delft with its medieval gates. Even the Prince of Orange had chosen to live in this fortified city during the Dutch fight to get free of Spanish control. Ordinary people like his father, once a weaver of cloth, prospered here. Wealthy travelers came to buy fine tapestries and ceramic dishes, to stroll along Delft's charming bridges, and to rest in fine inns like the one his father owned. His father had made the inn special by hanging many paintings on its walls. He was an art dealer. The best artists in the land brought their paintings into his inn to be displayed and sold to wealthy businessmen and travelers who stayed there (Wheelock 15).

Jan leapt from his bed, dressed quickly, and entered the dining area. There his father ate breakfast, surrounded by great works of art. These images were highly praised and admired by all who gazed at them. Jan stared at the painted scenes of his great city, mounted on the wall. He pondered the miracle of painting. A simple wooden plank turned into a picture of the city in all its dazzling detail and color by the hand of a single man! Did the artist need special hands? Jan Vermeer wanted to try his hand at it. He did, becoming a master painter at St. Luke's Guild. He married and inherited his father's inn and the business that went with it.

The love of the inn, the light that flowed into it and the people who moved through it were the themes of all Vermeer's works.

Project 25: Collagraph Print

GROUP #3 PRINTMAKING
- Printmaking tools
- Foam sheets
- Chipboard or cardboard (Group #1)
- Scissors and glue (Group #5)
- Drawing paper (Group #2)

STUDENT GALLERY

What kind of floor does the artist have in Vermeer's painting, "The Artist in His Studio" on page 64? Dutch floors were most often made of wooden planks, however many Dutch artists like Vermeer, painted a checkerboard pattern. They did this to add interest to the paintings. While being very careful to paint the details in some areas, they invented details in others! You can make a checkered floor and more using a collagraph print.

Use a piece of chipboard or cardboard as a base for the collagraph plate. Cut shapes from sheets of craft foam or the chipboard. Glue the pieces onto the cardboard base to make a picture. Allow to dry. The cut out shapes make a raised surface on the cardboard plate that catches the ink.

Have your adult helper set up a workspace with wax paper attached to the table surface with masking tape, as was done in previous printmaking projects. Create a space for inking the brayer and a space for your cardboard plate. Lay the finished cardboard plate face up on the wax paper. Place a piece of paper on top of the cardboard plate. You roll the brayer across the ink as before. Then, holding the edges down so that it does not slide, run the inked brayer over the top of the paper. Your print will appear.

Students use collagraph in a variety of subjects: sunflower, frog, and snake by Hannah, Katy, and Christina, all age 11. They used several ink colors on the wax paper. The colors mixed slightly as the brayer rolled over them.

Lesson 26

The Painter by Vermeer

Jan Vermeer's thirty-six known works all center on a single figure or small group placed in front of a window. Since he was the owner of an inn, we can assume that he was quite busy with the business of taking care of it. So his paintings were made there. Here we see a view of an artist painting. Many believe it is a picture of him. The model is placed in front of a window. Sunlight provides the source of light. Vermeer paints light on her blue satin dress, the wall, floor, the book she holds, the table, and the heavy curtain. Many remember Vermeer's paintings for capturing people in quiet moments, but we can also see that he captured something much more mysterious and that is the beauty of light.

Vermeer (van Delft), Jan (1632-1675) *The painter (Vermeer's self-portrait) and his model as Klio.* Oil on canvas, 1665-1666. 120 x 100 cm. Location: Kunsthistorisches Museum, Vienna, Austria Photo Credit: Erich Lessing / Art Resource, NY

An open door is like an invitation to come in. What does Vermeer use in this painting to invite us in? (The curtain is drawn back)
Where is the window in this painting? How do we know that it is there?
What objects does the model hold? Will they be a part of the artist's painting?

64

Project 26: Studio Drawing

> GROUP #5 Drawing
> Drawing paper
> Oil pastels

STUDENT GALLERY

This work is by Lindsey (age 9).

What do you see inside the places you work and live? Draw a scene of something you would see indoors using oil pastels. Oil pastels are similar to oil paints, but come in sticks.

Have you ever wondered why paintings from the 17th century are much darker than those we see today? When we know more about the places where art is made and the tools available to the artist, we can understand more about the art. A 17th century artist's studio was very dark, just like their homes. Since paintings were made indoors at this time, they were dark too. Candlelight was not very bright. They did not have electric lights. A window was the artist's only source of bright light. Windows were usually small because glass was expensive at that time.

Artists before the 17th century painted on hard surfaces like wooden panels or walls so that the paint would not crack. Once oil paint was discovered, artists could paint on canvas cloth stretched over a wooden frame, which is commonly used today. The flexible oil paint would not crack. Paintings were then more portable and could be carried around and put into any home or building after they were painted. Artists began painting pictures before they knew who would buy them or where they would be placed. This had a great effect on what kind of art was produced after the Renaissance (Filan, 40). An easel held the canvas upright while the artist painted his picture. Brushes were handmade using hog, squirrel, or otter hair. A bowl used to grind minerals and other substances into a powder for paint was called a mortar and a club-shaped tool for grinding or mashing substances was the pestle. A table of smooth stone created a surface for the stone muller, a heavy tool that was shaped like a cup turned upside-down. An assistant worked the muller around and around, pressing oil into the powdered pigments and coating each particle to make the oil paint smooth. A flat, circular piece of wood, called a palette, was held by the artist and used to mix colors while painting. These are just some of the things you would find in a seventeenth century studio.

Rococo Period   Lesson 27

Fragonard
Jean-Honore Fragonard,
Zhahn, aw naw RAY, fra gaw NAR,
(1732-1806)

The things that you grow up with can become things that you love through your whole life. Some people grow up with many animals and love them. Some people participate in sports as children and always have an interest in them. What do you do now or have now that you love? Can you imagine that you will love this during your whole life? Fragonard loved what most French men loved in the 1700's; clothing and other fine possessions.

Young Fragonard peeked into the window where his father worked as a haberdasher's assistant. His father held a tape, to measure the size of the gentleman who was being fitted for new breeches, justaucorps, and jacket. The haberdasher's store was filled with caps of all shapes and sizes, fancy stockings, ribbons to hold breeches in place, shoes with broad buckles, and an assortment of canes. It had everything a man needed to dress as a proper French gentleman in 1740. Clothing during Fragonard's time was of major importance. People sought the newest and finest clothing. It was highly decorated, just as you might imagine a fairy tale costume to be. Wearing fine clothing showed that a person was successful. Fragonard grew up to be a successful painter with a studio in the Louvre Palace.

People liked his paintings because they fit their joyful mood. He painted landscapes as soft and delicate places. Within those landscapes were young people in fine clothing. They amused themselves with games and laughter. The mood of the people who bought his work and supported him eventually changed as a new French ruler, Napoleon, came to power. Soon the new ruler's influence spread to the arts, so paintings of fun and pleasure were no longer in style. The new style was about power. Though Fragonard tried to make paintings in the new style, he could not change what was inside him. He would forever love of fine things in life: fine clothing, possessions, friends, and family.

Fragonard painted delicate, beautiful people and places. His paintings showed the luxury that the French people admired during the early part of his lifetime.

Project 27: Sculpt a Puppet

> GROUP #4 MODELING
> - Instant paper mache
> - Cardboard tube
> - Sock
> - Tempera paint, brush (Group #1)

STUDENT GALLERY

Ariel (age 9) made this puppet. You can make animal or people puppets by forming a head onto a cardboard tube.

Fragonard saw many customers come through the haberdasher's shop to get dressed up. You can dress up a puppet. Make a puppet head from paper mache and a body from the top of a sock. Decorate it with ribbons, threads, and other things you find. You may want to research what men and women wore in Fragonard's time, the 1700's.

Mix a small amount of paper mache with water according to its instructions. Cut a paper tube to be about three inches long or use a Dixie cup for the base. Build the paper mache head onto the base. Build a neck so that the head does not fall off the base. Allow it to dry completely. This will take two to three days depending on its thickness. When it is dry, paint the head with tempera paint. Allow the paint to dry. For clothing, use a single sock. Cut the toe off the sock. Cut small arm holes for your fingers to stick out of later. Glue the top edge onto the paper tube and allow the glue to dry.

Lesson 28

A Young Girl Reading by Fragonard

In this picture, we see a girl in a yellow dress. It is a simple silhouette, or side view. The beauty of this painting is the light. She sits facing a window and the light shines down onto the yellow dress, her face, and the book pages. The painting was first established using the dark brown tones that you see in the pillow and the back wall. Then the artist painted colors from the darkest to the lightest. It creates a truly striking and beautiful effect. Because this is an interior, it lacks all the lush green plant life that Fragonard puts in his outdoor scenes. This work is more quiet and peaceful.

Jean-Honore Fragonard, *A Young Girl Reading*, c. 1776.
Photo Credit: Dover Publications Inc.

We know that light stands out against a dark background. What light objects stand out from a dark background in this painting?

Where is the lightest part of the yellow dress?

Where is the lightest part of the pillow?

Hands can speak to us.
Does the girl hold the book awkwardly or delicately? The hands show the nature or character of the girl.

Project 28: Drawing People

GROUP #2 DRAWING
- Ebony pencil
- Drawing paper

STUDENT GALLERY

Anthony (age 10) made both of these student works.

Fragonard painted people as they played and enjoyed life in France. Watch people as they work or play. How do they move? Do the arms or legs bend? In what direction do they bend? Draw people using a pencil and show them in motion.

Look at the two drawings by Anthony. In the first drawing, he made the jumper's arms and legs stiff. In the second drawing, he draws the arms out instead of down and bends the jumper's legs. There is much more motion in this drawing.

Note to Adults: Students learn to draw more accurately when looking at real people. Here a student jumps the rope while two students turn. Other students draw from their observations of the movement. Adults can help students observe better by pointing things out. "Look at the way the jumper's legs bend. Can you draw them that way? Look at the ground. Can you make the people turning the rope stand on the ground so that we see the jumper is in the air?" In the first drawing, this student did not include these things. Always point to the action when showing corrections, and not to the picture itself. Let the student figure out how to resolve the problem.

Lesson 29

Romantic Period

Turner

Joseph Mallord William Turner, *Tur nur,* (1775-1851)

Have you ever experienced something so wonderful that you never forgot it? A thing we see, smell, or hear can stay with us for our entire lifetime. Turner painted so many glorious sunrises and sunsets throughout his lifetime that we must presume they were a special part of his life.

Joseph Turner opened the shop door and saw his father snipping at his customer's hair. He knew he would not assume his father's role as a barber. He would follow his own path. His painting had won a place in the exhibit at the Royal Academy and he would now become a student of art. Joseph called to his father, "Do you need help in the shop today, Father?"

His father looked up. "Not today Son. Go and prepare for your stay at the Academy." He placed some coins in Joseph's hands and gently pushed him out the door with an approving smile.

Joseph looked at the pile of coins that his father had given him. It would be enough to buy a proper suit of clothes and art supplies. It was a large sum. Joseph's mind raced with excitement. He would make it worth his father's sacrifice. He was not as wealthy as the other students were and he was much younger, but he felt he could do anything. After all, his studies with the mapmaker at age fifteen had paid off quickly. Those carefully measured drawings of buildings, including all the architectural details, were the perfect training for entrance into the Royal Academy. Joseph turned the street corner and the view hit him like a thunderbolt. The magnificent sky at sunset threw orange, red, pink and purple light on everything, like a painter had gone wild. It was the most glorious sight he had ever seen. "This is a sign of my good fortune," he declared aloud as he watched the sun sink below the horizon until every streak turned to deep blue.

Two years later Turner toured the countries of North Wales, Scotland, and Switzerland. He painted scenes of glorious sky, water, and land. By the middle of his career, he was focusing on light, especially the intense light of sunsets. He brushed thin glazes of color on top of one another and wiped them off with a cloth. Then he added dabs of paint suggesting ships, people, or clouds, often with a flat palette knife instead of a brush.

We can remember Turner for the way he painted light in the sky and on the water.

Project 29: Rubbings

GROUP #2 DRAWING
- Oil pastels
- Drawing paper
- Texture items shown below

Ships and steam locomotives were some of Turner's favorite subjects besides sunsets. He once had sailors tie him to the mast of a ship so that he could observe a storm more closely. He began to make paintings with heavy layers and texture in order to show wind, rain, and steam. You can make a textured picture too.

Create texture in your picture by rubbing your pastel over paper that sits on top of a textured surface. Place one sheet of drawing paper over a texture such as a crumpled piece of aluminum foil, sand paper, bubble wrap, or a group of coins. Peel half the covering off each oil pastel and rub the side of it over the paper. Experiment with different kinds of surfaces.

STUDENT GALLERY

This work of art was made by John (age 7). A close-up shows the texture on the octopus.

Here are some things we used to create a textured surface by rubbing. You might try a piece of wood, plaster wall, or a brick. Can you think of other objects that would make a texture?

Lesson 30

The Fighting Temeraire by Turner

Turner may have seen more in a sunset that most people do. He painted glimmering light, blending colors as he saw them each evening in the skies. His use of thick paint to show the colors in steam, storms, and sunlight conflicted with the way people thought a painting should look. They had judged a good work of art for the past 600 years by how detailed and real it looked. Still, they could not say that Turner's paintings didn't capture contemporary ideas. The message of this painting was clear. England's days of dominance at sea were over and the mighty little tugboat means that the Industrial Revolution is the new power. In this painting, we see the streaks of color both in the sky and on the surface of the water. Within the swirls of glorious light, the fighting Temeraire is being towed. Its sails are furled and only the masts and yardarms are seen. The large man-o-war, with three gun decks, is being retired from its long life as a battle ship. The steam powered tugboat pulls the ship forward, while the orange color of the sunset reflects in its large puff of steam.

Joseph Mallord William Turner (1775-1851) *The Fighting Temeraire*. Location: National Gallery, London, Great Britain Photo Credit: Art Resource, NY

What time of day has Turner chosen for this painting?
What colors does he use in the painting?
How does Turner paint the reflection of the ship and tugboat?

Project 30: Mixed Media
(Tissue Paper and Oil Pastels)

> GROUP #5 MIXED MEDIA
> - Cardboard, or chipboard (Group #1)
> - Brush (Group #1)
> - Tissue paper
> - Oil pastels (Group #2)
> - Glue

This work is by Ben (age 9).

In Turner's paintings, glazes (transparent washes of color) are layered on top of each other to create a colorful, hazy effect. You can create that effect by using colored tissue paper. Add oil pastels to finish the work. Think about scenes when you choose the colors of tissue paper. You could make a night scene using dark blues and whites for clouds. You could make a picture in sunset colors using yellows, orange, and red. You could make blue sky on top and green for grass below.

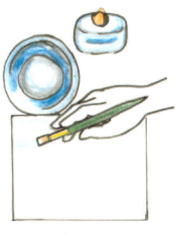

1. Prepare a paste solution by mixing two tablespoons of white glue with 1 tablespoon of water. Use construction paper or cardboard for the base. Cut tissue paper of various colors into strips.

2. Paste the tissue paper strips onto the cardboard using a brush. Overlap the colors. Brush glue over the surface to smooth rough areas once all tissue paper is in place.

3. Let the background dry. Then draw objects with oil pastels that complete the scene. You can trim the edges of the tissue paper with scissors.

Realist Period   Lesson 31

Millet
Jean-François Millet, mee LEH, (1814-1875)

Sometimes people move on to new places and better things only to find that what was familiar in their childhood was what they loved the most. Millet left his life on the farms of France to become a painter in the city of Paris. Later he returned to the French countryside and painted the life of the farmers that he knew and loved. He understood their hardships, their faith, and their perseverance and put these qualities into his paintings. Do you live in the country, a large city, or small town? What things do you like about the place you live?

Millet influenced future painters like Vincent van Gogh who made many copies of Millet's work like this one titled, *Sower* (after Millet); 1881. Photo Credit: Dover Publications Inc.

Millet's dream of escaping the harsh life of a farmer to become a painter had come true. He'd studied art at the most prestigious school in France, the Royal Academy of Painting and Sculpture. The school had started in 1648 to protect special artists and enlist their painting services for the country of France. Acceptance to this school soon became the only way an artist could make a successful career as a painter (Kren and Marx). After his training there, Millet had painted portraits for wealthy patrons for ten years, and he felt there might be better things to do with his talents. He sought a life of meaning, and his thoughts began to turn toward home again. He moved to Barbizon near the river of Fontainebleau. He loved the country and painted scenes from rural life. The flat land stretched out before him, and he chose to paint the field workers up close. In this way, their endless work was presented truthfully. The industrialists of France loved his new works. They were Socialists and wanted to promote the ideal of the hard worker in order to create a new social order to the government. Millet was not interested in politics or with changing the government. He said, "…the peasant subjects suit my temperament best; for I must confess, even if you think me a socialist, that the human side of art is what touches me most" (Getty). It would be this human side that would capture the interest of a new generation of artists: the Impressionists!

Millet's life in Barbizon caused him to create the Barbizon School. There he influenced a new generation of painters that would be called the Impressionists. They would change the way people thought about art forever.

Project 31: Watercolor Resist Painting

GROUP #1 PAINTING
- Watercolor paint set
- Watercolor paper
- Round brush
- Oil pastels (Group #2)

Look around you as Millet did when he painted the peasants working in the countryside of France. Draw something you see or have seen. Make a picture using watercolor resist.

STUDENT GALLERY

Jonathan (age 8) made this student work.

To make a watercolor resist, set up the painting area as shown in the picture. Set up paper, oil pastels, and watercolors.

With a black oil pastel stick, draw the outlines of your picture.

When the drawing is completed, paint into the spaces with watercolors. You can brush over the black outlines. The colors will not cover the lines even when you brush over them. The oil in the pastel resists the watercolor.

75

Lesson 32

The Gleaners by Millet

Millet painted the type of people that he knew as a child. In his paintings, you might see a laborer and his wife praying over their potato crop in the field or a single man sowing grain. This painting shows some of the poorest workers he knew. Women follow the harvest to gather any bits of grain that have fallen to the ground. They collect the grain in their aprons. The painting is arranged beautifully. The women are dressed in the modest clothing of peasants.

Jean-Franciois Millet, *The Gleaners*, 1857, Photo Credit: Dover Publications Inc.

What special colors does he use on the women's heads to get our attention?

What has Millet placed in the background that tells you about the place these women live and work in?

Do they live in a large city or a small community?

76

Project 32: Stand-up Sponge Painting

GROUP #5 MIXED MEDIA
- Construction paper
- Pencil, scissors, glue
- Sponge
- Tempera paint (Group #1)
- Paint brush (Group #1)
- Paper plate

Allison (age 9) made this student work. Stamps were used for the animals.

Millet painted the delicate stubble on the ground and other textures found outdoors. You can make a similar effect using a sponge. Follow the directions below.

1. Draw an outdoor scene. Draw objects onto colored construction paper. Include extra paper at the bottom of each object so that it can be folded and glued to the base.

2. Add foliage or leaves to objects like trees or bushes with a sponge. Wet the sponge and then wring it out before you start. Place tempera paint onto a paper plate. With a brush, add a little water to each color so that it is not stiff, but liquid. Dip the sponge into a small amount of the paint and dab it onto the trees or bushes to create the effect of leaves. Dip the sponge in two colors at once for a different effect. When you are done rinse the sponge immediately in warm water and store for future use.

3. Once the paint is dry, cut out the objects. Fold the bottom edge. Glue the bottom edge onto the base where you want it. The base can be painted and folded as well. You have created a stand-up sponge painting.

1. Draw

2. Sponge paint

3. Cut and glue

77

Congratulations in completing this art course. You have made art, using skills that all artists use. You explored European painting with famous artists who changed the way people thought about art. You studied a time when painting something to look real was highly valued and remained the most important idea in art. You learned about the great discoveries of the Renaissance artists and those that built upon their ideas and traditions.

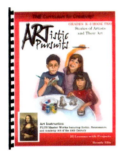

CONGRATULATIONS!

_____

has successfully completed *Artistic Pursuits, Grades K-3 Book 2 Stories of Artists and Their Art* on this day of

_____

Signed:

_____

Bibliography

Becherucci, Luisa. Raphael and Painting. *The Complete Work of Raphael.* Harrison House Publishers, 1969.

Filan, Kevin. *The Technical Revolution of Oil Painting.* Renaissance Magazine. Vol. 10 #2, Issue #42, 2005.

Getty Museum, The. *Jean-François Millet.* Retrieved January 22, 2008 from source: http://www.getty.edu/art/gettyguide/artMakerDetails?maker=588.

Hibbard, Howard. *Michelangelo.* New York, Hagerstown, San Francisco, London: Harper & Row, Publishers, 1974.

Molho, Anthony. Renaissance. *The World Book Encyclopedia.* Vol. 16 (pp.233). Chicago, London, Sydney, Toronto: World Book, Inc., 1994.

Owen, Chris. What is the Tre's Riches Heures? *Web Museum, Paris.* 1995. Retrieved June 10, 2002 from source: www.ibiblio.org/wm/rh/what.html.

Payne, Laura. *Essential History of Art.* UK: Parragon Publishing, 2000.

Pioch, Nicolas. Who Was Their Patron? *Web Museum, Paris.* 1995. Retrieved June 10, 2002 from source: www.ibiblio.org/wm/rh/patron.html.

Pioch, Nicolas. How Did They Paint the Tre's Riches Heures? *Web Museum, Paris.* 1995. Retrieved June 10, 2002 from source:www.ibiblio.org/wm/rh/how.html.

Pioch, Nicolas. Durer, Albrecht. *Web Museum, Paris.* 1995. Retrieved June 11, 2002 from source: www.ibiblio.org/wm/paint/auth/durer.

Rabiner, Donald. Giotto. *The World Book Encyclopedia.* Vol. 8 (pp.193). Chicago, London, Sydney, Toronto: World Book, Inc., 1994.

Roalf, Peggy. *Landscapes, Look at Paintings.* New York: Hyperion Books for Children, 1992.

Saitzyk, Steven L. *Art Hardware,* New York: Watson Guptill Publications, 1987.

Stone-Ferrier, Linda. Van Eyck. *The World Book Encyclopedia.* Vol. 20 (pp.306). Chicago, London, Sydney, Toronto: World Book, Inc., 1994.

Vasari, Giorgio. *The Lives of the Artists: a new translation by Julia Conaway Bondanella and Peter Bondanella,* Oxford World's Classics. Oxford, New York: Oxford University Press, 1998. First Published in 1550.

Wheelock, Jr. Arthur K. *Johannes Vermeer.* Washington: National Gallery of Art, and The Hague: Royal Cabinet of Paintings Mauritshuis, 1995.

Zafran, Eric M. Raphael. *The World Book Encyclopedia.* Vol. 16 (pp.142-143). Chicago, London, Sydney, Toronto: World Book, Inc., 1994.